T0259071

SURVEILLANCE AND THREAT DETECTION

SURVEILLANCE AND THREAT DETECTION

Prevention versus Mitigation

RICHARD KIRCHNER, JR.

AMSTERDAM • BOSTON • HEIDELBERG • LONDON
NEW YORK • OXFORD • PARIS • SAN DIEGO
SAN FRANCISCO • SINGAPORE • SYDNEY • TOKYO
Butterworth-Heinemann is an imprint of Elsevier

Acquiring Editor: Brian Romer
Development Editor: Marisa LaFleur
Project Manager: Priya Kumaraguruparan
Designer: Matthew Limbert

Butterworth-Heinemann is an imprint of Elsevier
225 Wyman Street, Waltham, MA 02451, USA
The Boulevard, Langford Lane, Kidlington, Oxford OX5 1GB UK

Notices
Knowledge and best practice in this field are constantly changing. As new research and
experience broaden our understanding, changes in research methods or professional practices,
may become necessary. Practitioners and researchers must always rely on their own experience
and knowledge in evaluating and using any information or methods described herein. In using
such information or methods they should be mindful of their own safety and the safety of
others, including parties for whom they have a professional responsibility.

To the fullest extent of the law, neither the Publisher nor the authors, contributors, or editors,
assume any liability for any injury and/or damage to persons or property as a matter of products
liability, negligence or otherwise, or from any use or operation of any methods, products,
instructions, or ideas contained in the material herein.

Library of Congress Cataloging-in-Publication Data
Application submitted

British Library Cataloging-in-Publication Data
A catalogue record for this book is available from the British Library

ISBN: 978-0-12-407780-5

For information on all Butterworth-Heinemann
publications visit our web site at store.elsevier.com

Printed and bound in United States of America
14 15 16 17   10 9 8 7 6 5 4 3 2 1

 **Working together
to grow libraries in
developing countries**

www.elsevier.com • www.bookaid.org

CONTENTS

CONTENTS

DIGITAL ASSETS

Thank you for selecting Butterworth Heine-
mann's *Surveillance and Threat Detection*. To
complement the learning experience, we have
provided a number of online tools to accompany
this edition. Two distinct packages of interactive
digital assets are available: one for instructors
and one for students.

Please consult your local sales representative
with any additional questions.

For the Instructor

Qualified adopters and instructors need to
register at the this link for access: http://
textbooks.elsevier.com/web/manuals.aspx?isbn=
9780124077805

- **Test Bank** Compose, customize, and deliver
  exams using an online assessment package
  in a free Windows-based authoring tool that
  makes it easy to build tests using the unique
  multiple choice and true or false questions
  created for *Surveillance and Threat Detection*.
  What's more, this authoring tool allows you to
  export customized exams directly to Black-
  board, WebCT, eCollege, Angel and other
  leading systems. All test bank files are also
  conveniently offered in Word format.
- **PowerPoint Lecture Slides** Reinforce key
  topics with focused PowerPoints, which
  provide a perfect visual outline with which
  to augment your lecture. Each individual

book chapter has its own dedicated slideshow.
- **Instructor's Guides** Design your course around customized learning objectives, discussion questions, and other instructor tools.

For the Student

Students will need to visit this link in order to access the ancillaries below. http://www.elsevierdirect.com/companion.jsp?ISBN=9780124077805

- **Self-Assessment Question Bank** Enhance review and study sessions with the help of this online self-quizzing asset. Each question is presented in an interactive format that allows for immediate feedback.
- **Case Studies** Apply what is on the page to the world beyond with the help of topic-specific case studies, each designed to turn theory into practice and followed by interactive scenario-based questions that allow for immediate feedback.

ACKNOWLEDGMENTS

In the course of the writing and research for this book, if I have failed to directly acknowledge the specific words of those who have written them, then it is not my intent to represent those words as my own and I happily provide acknowledgment to those who were original in their thoughts.

Portions of this book were written through the expert writing of Mark Graham and Mario Acevedo of Mark Graham Communications, Denver, Colorado. Thank you, gentlemen.

A special thank you to every member of the Pentagon Force Protection Agency–Office of Threat Detection past and present, particularly Ken "Mad Dog" Maddrey and Chaka Smith; Mr. Jim Pelkofski; the PFPA CI Shop; my friend(s) at the Threat Management Unit–CIA; John Reale for his cheerleading and keen business insights; Dan Botsch (and his professional staff) of TrapWire, Inc.; the Hon. George P. Shultz; editor extraordinaire Mary Jane Peluso with honorable mention to Amber Hodge for her latitude with deadlines; my loving parents; then oldest to youngest—Taddy, Sean, Skyelar, Liam, Emma, Christopher, and Lauren; and a very special thank you to my wife Kathleen, who, over and above the mothering of the aforementioned seven, is always at my side and shows me all things are possible through faith and our true love.

PREFACE AND INTRODUCTION

CHAPTER OUTLINE

Abstract: *Surveillance and Threat Detection Methodology* is the most definitive resource to date addressing threat detection and attack prevention. This book contains never-before-published information from a subject-matter expert in the growing field of threat detection. The author shares a wealth of practical information on surveillance detection in the physical security realm. You are offered the opportunity to recognize a paradigm shift in modern-day security—one that goes from the reactive to the proactive—with details on how to protect yourself from terrorist and criminal attacks *before* they reach your doorstep! You will learn how to train your security force with the techniques and tactics necessary to recognize hostile surveillance and thwart an attack. This book is ideal for the professional physical security officer who wants a tooth-to-tail understanding of surveillance and threat detection.

Keywords: audience, detection, deterrence, normal, surveillance, territory, threat

1.1 Definitions

Actionable information: Information that is directly useful to customers for immediate exploitation without having to go through the full intelligence production process.

Anarchist: A person who rebels against any authority, established order, or ruling power.

Countersurveillance: All measures, active or passive, taken to counteract hostile surveillance.

Criminal enterprise: All illegal activity committed.

Emotionally disturbed persons: Individuals found within an administrative site assessed as either temporarily or permanently psychologically or mentally impaired to a degree that the person is gravely disabled or presents a clear danger to that person or another.

Foreign intelligence entity: Any foreign organization, person, or group (public, private, governmental) that conducts intelligence activities to acquire U.S. information, block or impair U.S. intelligence collection, influence U.S. policy, or disrupt U.S. systems and programs. This term includes a foreign intelligence and security service.

Hostile civil disturbance entities: Identified organizations known to target Department of Defense personnel, facilities, and assets through violence and other destructive and disruptive means.

If You See Something, Say Something: Trademarked public access program for individual reporting of suspicious activity to law enforcement.

Illegal imaging: The act of taking photos or recording video footage without prior authorization as outlined in jurisdictional law.

Measuring: Actively measuring distances of physical locations or objects by individuals located at that site through simple pacing, ground still photography, and/or commercially obtained overhead still photography. Measuring is a key step in the planning phase of attack/exploitation cycles, as the collection of such information assures the accuracy of plans, logistics, and execution.

Observation: Also regarded as "physical surveillance," this is systematic and deliberate observation of a person by any means on a continuing basis or acquisition of a nonpublic communication by a person not a party thereto or visibly present threat through any means not involving electronic surveillance.

Operational security: A protective and proactive discipline implemented to mitigate the risk of inadvertent exposure of personnel, methods, and means falling under surveillance detection (SD) purview. SD ensures and manages the continuous implementation of this discipline as to safeguard assigned personnel from potential negative or lethal actions having terrorism, antigovernment, foreign intelligence, and/or criminal nexus.

Presidential Executive Order 12333: President Ronald Reagan signed Presidential Executive Order 12333 on December 4, 1981 (U.S. President 1981, 1). The directive delineated the duties and responsibilities of the various U.S. intelligence agencies. This directive was also designed to protect the United States, its national interests and citizens, from foreign security threats. It also prohibited assassinations by stating, "No person employed by or acting on behalf of the United States Government shall engage in, or conspire to engage in, assassination" (U.S. President 1981, 18).

Querying: The acquisition of information from a person or group in a manner that does not disclose the intent of the interview or conversation. A technique of human source intelligence collection, generally overt, unless the collector is other than he or she purports to be.

Surveillance: The systematic observation of aerospace, surface, or subsurface areas, places, persons, or things by visual, aural, electronic, photographic, or other means.

Surveillance detection: Measures taken to detect and/or verify whether an individual, vehicle, or location is under surveillance.

Surveillance operation specialist: These personnel possess specialized advanced skills, training, and experiences in surveillance, surveillance detection, and countersurveillance methodologies.

Suspicious activity: Observed behavior indicative of criminal activities, intelligence gathering, or other preoperational planning related to national security or public safety.

Terrorism: The unlawful use of violence or threat of violence to instill fear and coerce governments and/or societies. Terrorism is often motivated by religious, political, or other ideological beliefs and is committed in the pursuit of goals that are usually political.

Terrorist-related suspicious activity: Observed behavior consistent with preoperational targeting relating to a potential terrorist threat(s) to national security interests. Furthermore, any activity or behavior related to planning, preparation (including probes), and attack execution.

Test of security: Any attempt to measure reaction times and actions by police, security personnel, and/or other first responders. A simple mistake such as a vehicle approaching a security barrier and then turning around or an attempt to circumvent access control procedures in order to assess strengths and weaknesses of police and equipment can disguise acts of test of security.

Timing: A subset of observation or "physical surveillance" with the intent of identifying the precise moment in which gaps of security appear; associated patterns of life or reoccurring patterns set by individuals of interest, assets, and critical mission functions. Adversarial planners require this information in support of the analysis, collection management, and dissemination targeting cycle.

1.2 Scope

Surveillance and Threat Detection Methodology is the most definitive resource to date addressing threat detection and attack prevention. This book contains never-before-published information from a subject-matter expert in the growing field of threat detection. The author shares a wealth of practical information on surveillance detection in the physical security realm. You are offered the opportunity to recognize a paradigm shift in modern-day security—one that goes from the reactive to the proactive—with details on how to protect yourself from terrorist and criminal attacks *before* they reach your doorstep! You will learn how to train your security force with the techniques and tactics necessary to recognize hostile surveillance and thwart an attack. This book is ideal for the professional physical security officer who wants a tooth-to-tail understanding of surveillance and threat detection.

The persistent stream of suspicious activity reports is proof that the "bad guys" are conducting surveillance of valuable targets in the United States and abroad. Such surveillance indicates preattack planning by terrorists and criminals and demands attention by security officers at all levels. To stop these attacks, security officers must understand terrorist and criminal surveillance and planning—to know what the "bad guys" are looking for and how they gather intelligence. Key to this understanding is that security officers learn how to distinguish "normal" from "not normal" behavior that will alert you to hostile surveillance and preattack planning. With this knowledge, security officers can implement protective countermeasures to detect, deter, disrupt, and defend against future attacks.

Whether you are responsible for a local storage facility, a bank, a mass-transit depot, or a nuclear reactor, introduction of a proactive threat detection program will increase your chances of preventing any attack dramatically. Such a program will align your security assets precisely to where they are needed and give you the tools to recognize if you are the target of criminal or terrorist surveillance. This first edition includes a historical overview of surveillance and an in-depth analysis of terrorist preattack and attack methodologies—illustrated with relevant real-world case studies. It describes how to incorporate threat detection into both a fixed-site physical security program and toward the protection of high-risk personnel. It discusses the counterintelligence and business intelligence arena and reviews the latest technologies in threat detection and how they may integrate into your operations.

You will come to understand preattack and attack surveillance methodology and, more importantly, learn how to recognize hostile surveillance so you can *prevent* an attack.

1.3 Audience and Use Case Assumptions

For most of the individuals in the security and force protection ecosystem, "surveillance detection" is used commonly to describe the act of taking measures to detect and/or verify whether an individual, vehicle, or location is under surveillance. Throughout this book the words "threat detection" are utilized with and in place of "surveillance detection," as surveillance detection fails to capture the full scope of threats; threat detection fully encompasses the entire process of recognizing "threat" not just "surveillance." With many years working on and around the U.S. Pentagon Reservation we were looking for the enemy we wanted (Al Qaida, Hezbollah, Lone Wolves, etc.), yet we found the enemy we had (Russia, China, emotionally disturbed persons, etc.) all "threats" in and of themselves. This methodology rests on the proven historical understanding that the common element across the threat spectrum—regardless if it's internationally state-sponsored actors, homegrown violent extremists, extremist militia groups, intelligence operations, everyday criminals, or the emotionally disturbed person—has been, and will continue to be, that bad actors routinely observe and record their target's activities to discover vulnerabilities and collect preoperational attack intelligence.

It should also be explained that the term "surveillance detection" is a misnomer. The word *surveillance* is the French word for "watching over"; "sur" means "from above" and "veiller" means "to watch." The word *surveillance* may be applied to observation from a distance by means of electronic equipment [such as closed-circuit television (CCTV) cameras] and usually of people for the purpose of influencing, managing, directing, or protecting. Therefore, detecting surveillance or "surveillance detection" could infer simply looking up to see a CCTV camera. The inverse of surveillance is sousveillance ("to watch from below") or the recording of an activity from the perspective of a participant in that activity or from ground level by an individual actor or even a small group. This is more to what threat detection methodology is seeking to discover, as this is the norm for bad actors collecting attack intelligence. However, and furthermore, simply looking for sousveillance is only a part of the requirement to capture actors conducting hostile preplanning and preoperational activity. The full spectrum of the threat (i.e., probing, querying, dry runs, and signaling) must be included to better define this evolving security strategy.

Threat detection programs are designed to exploit these risks by creating a mechanism to detect preoperational surveillance, report sightings, and disrupt an attack. The full threat detection program outlined in this book may not be conducive to all organizations. Parts of the program can be extracted and suited to the needs of each organization's security plan. Before developing a threat detection program, organizations should ensure that their program will be in legal accordance with host country laws.

Disclaimer: The contents of this book are to provide rudimentary threat detection methodologies, much of which can be found as an open source with research. It is not intended as an advanced practical guide. To make such a textbook on advanced practices available publicly would certainly be studied by nefarious actors and would not be in the best interest of national public security. It is recommended for security practitioners that recognize the security and business value of threat detection, and desire a full scope program, to reach out to threat detection professionals for one-on-one consultations.

1.4 Executive Summary

Stopping attacks by terrorists and criminals against federal, state, local government, and corporate targets must include a new and proactive approach: *prevention* through the identification and disruption of preattack planning and surveillance activities. Because terrorists and criminals must conduct surveillance of their intended targets—often over a period of weeks, months, or even years—the detection of suspicious events and the correlation of these events can reveal the threat of an impending attack.

Surveillance and Threat Detection Methodology provides one of the most effective protective measures to prevent such an attack and does so by offering a paradigm shift in security thinking—one that is *proactive* versus *reactive*. This book shows how proactive measures can detect hostile surveillance and *prevent* an attack. Security officers will be taught the systematic steps of the criminal and terrorist preattack methodology and learn how to recognize suspicious behavior that signals preattack surveillance and planning. Incredibly, most in the public and private security industries have never heard of this methodology and so do not understand how to institute such a preventative program. With the information in this book, security officers can learn how to identify "bad guys" and employ appropriate countermeasures. This information encompasses how to detect terrorist and criminal surveillance and preattack planning, analyze suspicious activity reports, and develop an effective threat detection program. The results will increase the probability of preventing an attack dramatically while streamlining protection assets and costs.

The current model used to portray the security and protection of a facility is as concentric circles of physical security. In this model, we think of hardening the facility to provide warning and defend against an attack. The outermost ring represents where we would first detect a threat and adopt a heightened security posture. Security at this outer ring would be provided by long-range observation from within the facility and by patrolling the surrounding area. The middle ring represents where we begin screening access to the facility. Entry into the facility would be channeled for control. It is here that we would rely on CCTV and active surveillance by security officers. The inner ring represents detection devices and physical barriers, such as metal detectors, alarms, dogs, fences, bollards, Jersey barriers, and guards to prevent unauthorized entry into the facility. The problem with this model is that it is reactive to a threat. Terrorists and criminals will surveil your facility to find the vulnerabilities in your security measures and penetrate even the most hardened of perimeters.

A better model is to think of security as concentric models of suspicious behavior. In the outermost ring, terrorists and criminals conduct cursory surveillance of your facility. At this point, their objective is twofold: (1) to see if an attack on your facility meets their strategic goal and (2) to gauge your facility's protective measures. Is it a hard or a soft target? The bad guys will engage in very-low profile behaviors as they observe your facility. They may simply walk by, watch, and take notes. If terrorist and criminals decide that an attack on your facility would still meet their strategic goal, then they will adopt more aggressive behaviors to gather intelligence; that is, they will move into the middle ring of suspicious behavior. Expect extensive documentation using photography, video, and hand-drawn maps. The bad guys will scout for surveillance zones where they can linger and observe unobtrusively. They will gain detailed information about your "pattern of life" and report the findings to their high-level operatives. If your facility has been designated as the target, then expect even more aggressive behaviors from the surveillants as they move into the inner ring of suspicious behavior. Keep in mind that the bad guys will be clever in their methods, as they do not want to get caught and compromise their mission. They seek to get as much information as they can about the vulnerabilities of your security measures and to gauge the ability to meet their attack objectives (inflict maximum causalities, destroy the building, break into the vault, etc.). At this point, they will confront your security officers personally to ask questions, test your defenses and responses, gain entry into your facility, and find the lapses and gaps in your security measures. On the eve of the attack—the bull's eye of our rings of suspicious behavior—the bad guys will be present in full force to conduct last-minute surveillance and dress rehearsals to assure a successful operation, despite physical defenses.

1.4.1 Why Threat Detection

1.4.1.1 Territorial Dominance

When humans have their own territory, there is an impulse to defend this territory against others seeking to "invade" it. Territoriality is the attempt by an individual or group to affect, influence, or control people, phenomena, and relationships by delimiting and asserting control over a geographic area.[1]

1.4.1.2 Territorial Integrity

Your organization should *own* its operating environment and defend its territory effectively against acts of violence by another. KIRIK's

---

[1] Robert D. Sack. *Human Territoriality: Its Theory and History* (Cambridge Studies in Historical Geography). Cambridge University Press, November 1986.

Systematic Attack Prevention threat detection program of training law enforcement and security builds systematic and sustained territorial dominance.

1.4.1.3 Territorial Imperative

Every criminal and terrorist attack is preceded by hostile operational surveillance. KIRIK's Systematic Attack Prevention threat detection program identifies these indicators through the force-multiplying effect of training ground protective forces in recognizing these indicators.

1.4.1.4 Territorial Intelligence

Still, incoming data of suspicious activity are just information. In order to be an effective protective force, organizations must make the relationship with these data actionable. This now becomes intelligence—real, or near real-time, actionable intelligence.

Again, your organization should *own* its operating environment and defend its territory effectively against acts of violence by another.

This book is the first of its kind and will attract a substantial audience of security officers eager to improve their posture against attack. As the understanding of this surveillance and threat detection methodology emerges over the next decade, this book's proactive measures will become the standard of the physical security industry.

Upon conclusion, the readers will understand the terrorist/criminal cycle and, more importantly, how to interrupt that cycle to *prevent* an attack. Readers have real-world case studies to draw from that apply to their real-world security responsibilities. Readers will understand how threat detection at a high-value fixed site facility can be integrated into an overall security footprint for any organization.

Almost all training programs designed to protect assets from become targets of terrorism and other criminal activities discuss the need to be vigilant for individuals conducting surveillance. Unfortunately, this advice is woefully insufficient and typically passed over due to most people and organizations having had no training or experience in how to detect hostile surveillance. Today's security posture is to harden the target with guns, gates, and guards—or deterrence. This has proven and continues to be an effective method for protecting assets. Nevertheless, it is only half of what should be in place to protect your assets. Detection is the other half.

Incorporating a robust threat detection program and further fully integrating such a program into your daily current operations dramatically improves your security posture over and above the guns, gates, and guards that are simply surrounding your asset waiting for the attack to arrive. As you wait for the attack to come, with each passing day of no security event at your location, you and those you protect are a day closer to the next disastrous event. Yes, following September 11, 2001, the United States has done a good job of sharing information, bolstering response capabilities across multiple jurisdictions, agencies, and first responders. Creation of the National Incident Management System has made us all better responders to incident. But, in affect, what we are now are better victims for the next attack.

Building concentric circles of security around us and *hoping* we are not being targeted is not a completely sound security program. *Hope* is not a strategic plan.[2] Initialization and standardization of a threat detection capability provide you, the security practitioner, real-time ground intelligence and awareness of what is occurring at your location.

$$Detection + Deterrence = Defeat$$

---

[2] Brigadier General Jonathon H. Cofer, Principal Deputy Director, Pentagon Force Protection Agency.

OVERVIEW AND UNDERSTANDING

Abstract: In history, surveillance is often referred to as spying or espionage. Most often, surveillance occurred historically as a means to gather and collect information, supervise the actions of other people (usually enemies), and use this information to increase one's understanding of the party being spied on.

Keywords: analyze, document, collate, history, identify, share, surveillance zone

2.1 Historical Overview of Surveillance, Countersurveillance, and Surveillance Detection

In history, surveillance is often referred to as spying or espionage. Most often, surveillance occurred historically as a means to gather and collect information, supervise the actions of other people (usually enemies), and use this information to increase one's understanding of the party being spied on.

During biblical and ancient times, surveillance occurred most often through use of an individual spy, or a small group of spies. As technology such as spyglasses, telescopes, and radios developed, surveillance technologies continually affected the way in which surveillance occurred. Modern surveillance technologies such as closed-circuit television (CCTV), radio frequency identification, and global positioning systemshelp highlight the extent to which surveillance practices have evolved throughout history.

As Keith Laidler proposes in his book *Surveillance Unlimited: How We've Become the Most Watched People on Earth*, "spying and surveillance are at least as old as civilization itself. The rise of city states and empires [...] meant that each needed to know not only the disposition and morale of their enemy, but also the loyalty and general sentiment of their own population."

There are many possible examples of surveillance found in the Bible. One example found is in the second book of Samuel—that of

David and Bathsheba. David, while walking on the roof of his palace, noticed Bathsheba bathing and as he continued to watch her his desire grew, even though she was already the wife of Uriah. In this example, surveillance was used for David's own personal gains and pleasure rather than for a greater good.

Another example, as noted by Keith Laidler, can be found in the book of Numbers. Here, "details of the information that the spies were required to collect" mostly regarding the land, how many people live on the land, the layout of the towns, the quality of the soil and the presence of trees (Numbers 13:17–20). Unlike the story of David and Bathsheba, surveillance here is being used for very different means. By collecting information regarding the people and the land, the spies would have been able to determine the strengths and weaknesses of their enemies. This use of surveillance satisfies one of the most basic characteristics of surveillance historically as well as modernly.

According to Terry Crowdy in his book *The Enemy Within: A History of Espion*age, "the earliest surviving record of espionage dates from the time of Pharaoh Rameses' war with the Hittites and the battle of Kadesh (c. 1274 BC)." The Hittite king Muwatallis sent two spies into the Egyptian camp posing as deserters to convince the pharaoh that the Hittite army was still quite distant. Rameses believed their story and unwittingly allowed part of his army to march into a Hittite ambush. Fortunately for the pharaoh, he captured two more Hittite spies and had his officers interrogate them. The Hittites spies revealed that an ambush had been set.

Ramses was therefore able to bring up reserves and avert disaster at what became known as the battle of Kadesh. Crowdy makes an important point by recognizing the fact that the precedent for altering general surveillance practices occurred very early on in history. Although spies are most often "known as collectors of information, they are often used to disseminate false information in order to deliberately mislead opponents."

2.1.1 Ancient Times

Since our days as prehistoric hunters, humans have always had a need for surveillance. Our ancestors observed and studied their prey as they planned and executed the hunt. Early humans no doubt used surveillance when they raided one another's camps to rob provisions, take prisoners, or chase rivals away from valuable land. Later, as people organized into larger communities, conflicts between competing tribes and nations evolved into warfare, and surveillance developed more sophisticated forms of gathering intelligence to include espionage.

Throughout history, rulers have relied on surveillance to collect intelligence on their enemies and to keep tab on their competitors. In the Bible (Numbers 13:17–20), Moses ordered spies to (1) surveil Canaan and bring back a rather detailed report that included the disposition and numbers of the populace, their fortifications, and the condition of the land and (2) to return with samples of their crops. The Chinese military philosopher Sun-Tzu and his Indian counterpart, Chanakya, discussed espionage in their writings. The ancient Greeks and Romans used spies. In feudal Japan, warlords and emperors hired ninjas for clandestine surveillance. The Mongols preceded their invasions with extensive surveillance.

The Aztecs relied on traveling merchants to report on their empire and its citizens. Queen Elizabeth I of England employed a sophisticated network of spies to apprise her of sedition, assassination attempts, and planned invasion. Her agents gathered intelligence using techniques of espionage that included phony letter drops, deciphering coded messages, and the interception of mail.

2.1.2 Use of Surveillance in War

Since watching an enemy to learn his intentions and secrets would present a significant advantage during war, nations have always relied on hostile surveillance.

During the American Revolutionary War, surveillance and espionage were used commonly by both sides. Scouts, rangers, and cavalry surveiled enemy lines. Colonial spies included Thomas Knowlton, the heralded martyr Nathan Hale, and the African-American double agent James Armistead. The most well-known British spy was John Andre, who was captured with correspondence from Benedict Arnold, then tried, and executed by hanging.

In the U.S. Civil War, surveillance and espionage were again common methods used to gain a military advantage. Scouts and cavalry provided surveillance on the battlefield, while spies gathered intelligence on troop and supply movements, military developments, and political intrigue. The federal government contracted the Pinkerton National Detective Agency to provide surveillance and countersurveillance work. The Pinkertons formalized the use of tradecraft to include shadowing and working undercover. The Confederates relied on spies such as Isabella Maria Boyd, who not only gathered military intelligence, but also collected information on the private lives of Washington high officials, which she used as leverage to secure her release from prison.

During the Boer War, Robert Baden-Powell, the founder of the Boy Scouts, surveilled enemy encampments and disguised his drawings of their fortifications within innocuous-appearing sketches of butterflies.

World War I was rife with covert surveillance on all sides. Factories, railroads, and harbors were vulnerable to hostile surveillance. The reliance on sea cargo made intelligence on merchant ships especially important for attack by surface raiders and submarines. "Loose lips sink ships" became a famous catch phrase to guard against the careless disclosure of classified information. The ability to intercept secret message traffic from correspondence, telegraph, or telephone became a valued skill. T.E. Lawrence, the renowned desert fighter, surveilled Ottoman military bases under the guise as an archeologist and later used Arab tribesmen for reconnaissance and espionage against the Turks.

Frederick Russell Burnham hid surveillance tools in his wooden leg during his work as a French spy against the Germans. The British secret agent Sidney George Reilly became the inspiration for Ian Fleming's super spy, James Bond. Probably the most famous of all the war's spies was Margaretha Geertruida Zelle, who performed as the exotic dancer *Mata Hari* and became known as the epitome of the femme fatale. Mata Hari spied for the Germans and was later arrested, tried, and executed by the French.

In World War II, the use of informants familiar with their native land was a great asset for surveillance. Citizens sympathetic to the Nazi cause were crucial in undermining Norwegian resistance. Inside occupied Europe and the conquered nations of the Pacific and Asia, informants provided the allies with valuable information to help defeat the Germans and Japanese. Espionage was raised to a high art, employing well-trained professional agents equipped with gadgets such as sophisticated lock picks, miniature cameras, and secret radios. Countersurveillance was stressed to safeguard the military effort and deny the enemy intelligence. Factories providing war material instituted strict security measures to prevent espionage and sabotage.

The Cold War was a time of intense surveillance between the United States and the USSR. Both sides developed and employed a wide variety of methods, ranging from high-altitude reconnaissance airplanes, satellites, submarines, snooping devices, spies, and informants.

2.1.3 Terrorist Surveillance

Preoperational surveillance is a critical component for every terrorist or criminal attack. Given that the purpose of hostile surveillance is to observe, document, and analyze the target security measures, patterns, and vulnerabilities, surveillance can be the most visible step in the attack-planning process. Therefore, surveillance involves the most risk for attackers.

Preoperational surveillance is critical to every attack. Terrorists began conducting preoperational surveillance for over 2 years before the November 2008 Mumbai attacks took place. The coordinated, multitarget attacks involved detailed planning and long-term hostile surveillance. On multiple occasions the terrorists entered at least one of the Mumbai target locations and posed as a patron. Additionally, terrorists stayed at a hotel that was very close and in the line of sight to the locations they planned to attack. In all, there were at least six surveillance trips to the various attack targets.

On average, the terrorist cells held their first planning meetings slightly over 3 months from the time they committed the terrorist incidents studied. This is generally consistent with Rapoport's (1992) notion that terrorist groups have a life expectancy of less than 1 year. The life span of these "cells" ranged from a few weeks to more than 3 years.

The initial "planning phase" appears to last, on average, from 12 days to approximately 2 months. It is during this period that law enforcement agencies would have the greatest probability of successful intervention. Planning and preparatory activities cannot be separated temporally. Meetings, preparation, training, and procurement of materials for terrorist incidents are not sequenced independent of each other. Substantial variation among types of terrorist groups (e.g., single-issue, international) regarding this issue was apparent. However, the limited amount of temporal data available from these case studies precludes further specification than the overall pattern of conduct.

The onset of preparatory behavior typically began about 3 to 4 months prior to the planned terrorist incident. Preparatory conduct may include criminal as well as noncriminal activity. The most common preparatory behaviors included meetings, phone calls, purchase of supplies and materials, and banking activities, which included everything from a bank robbery to fund the planned incident to legitimate withdrawals.

Terrorist groups engaged in an average of 2.3 known behaviors per incident. Further examination, however, revealed that one-fourth (115 of 453; 25.3%) of these activities were "ancillary"—predominately criminal conduct associated with the terrorist group that could have been used as a "preincident indicator," but which was not related directly to the planning of the eventual terrorist incident. Of the 453 behaviors recorded, nearly one-third (145 of 453; 32.1%) involved a criminal offense. The most common of these crimes involved acquiring, manufacturing, or testing bombs (24 of 145; 16.6%). Conspiracies do not frequently become known to law enforcement agencies until after the completion of the act or other arrests are made. Consequently, nonovert acts of conspiracies, such as meetings and phone calls, may not come to the attention of local law enforcement agencies. However, three-fourths of these crimes involved "observable" offenses, which might lead the police to suspicion more sinister activities. Robbery (21 of 145; 14.4%), murder (9 of 145; 6.1%), and training (9 of 145; 6.1%) constituted the remaining most common preparatory and ancillary offenses committed.

Once preparations for the terrorist act have been completed, overall analysis suggests a lull between final acts of preparation and commission of the terrorist act. On average, the terrorist incident occurred or was scheduled to occur between 3 and 6 weeks following the final known act in preparation. In fact, this average time would have been much shorter except for the existence of a few outliers where preparatory behaviors near the time of the incident were not known. Among cases where preparatory acts were measured, nearly two-thirds (65.2%) of the terrorist incidents involved a preparatory act on the day of the incident and another 9% of the groups committed their last preparatory act the day prior to the incident.

While generalizations based these data are risky due to low representativeness and small sample size, the overall pattern appears to be that the planning process is relatively short—3 to 4 months prior to the commission of an incident. Planning and preparation occur concurrently during this period and seem to be characterized by surveillance and meetings. Known preparatory behaviors conclude 3 to 6 weeks prior to the incident, followed by a lull in activity prior to the date of the incident.[1]

---

[1] *Pre-Incident Indicators of Terrorist Incidents: The Identification of Behavioral, Geographic, and Temporal Patterns of Preparatory Conduct.* Authors: Brent L. Smith and Kelly R. Damphousse.

2.1.4 Counterintelligence Surveillance

Although some trace the origins of spying to the time of Moses in the Bible, many experts point out the contributions of the ancient spy master, Sun Tzu (500 BC). American history traces spying to the American Revolution. Espionage, counterintelligence (CI), and covert action have been important tools of U.S. political leaders since the founding of the Republic.

Counterintelligence is any effort to protect secrets, prevent an intelligence mechanism from being manipulated, and exploit the intelligence activities of another entity. It can be passive or active. Passive or defensive CI is called "security" and involves locating, screening, and identifying people; limiting their access to classified material; and instituting accounting systems to trace losses. Active CI is called "countermeasures" and involves specific protections using specific tactics such as neutralizing an enemy or putting them under surveillance.

During the Revolutionary War, General George Washington and patriots such as Benjamin Franklin and John Jay directed a broad range of clandestine operations that helped the colonies win independence. They ran networks of agents and double agents, employed deceptions against the British army, launched sabotage operations and paramilitary raids, used codes and ciphers, and disseminated propaganda and disinformation to influence foreign governments. America's founders all agreed with General Washington that "the necessity of procuring good intelligence is apparent and need not be further argued." Nathan Hale, of course, was America's most famous spy, and everyone knows his famous quote in 1776 when he was about to be hanged: "I only regret that I have but one life to lose for my country."

Presidents in the early republic were involved actively in intelligence activities, especially covert actions. In his first State of the Union message, Washington requested that Congress establish a "secret service fund" for clandestine activities. Within 2 years, the fund represented over 10% of the federal budget. Thomas Jefferson drew on it to finance the first covert attempt of the United States to topple a foreign government, one of the Barbary Pirate states, in 1804–1805 (it failed). James Madison employed agents of influence and clandestine paramilitary forces to acquire territory in the Florida region from Spain during 1810–1812. Several presidents dispatched undercover agents on espionage missions overseas. One spy, disguised as a Turk, obtained a copy of a treaty between the Ottoman Empire and France. Also during this period, Congress tried to exercise oversight of the secret fund, but President James K. Polk rebuffed the lawmakers, saying "The experience of every nation on earth has demonstrated that emergencies may arise in which it becomes absolutely necessary ... to make expenditures, the very object of which would be defeated by publicity" (the Polk Doctrine).

There is a widely held conception that terrorist surveillance is generally sophisticated and almost invisible, but in actuality, it is discovered frequently that individuals who conduct terrorist surveillance tend to be quite sloppy and sometimes even amateurish in their surveillance tradecraft. There are some exceptions, of course.

Many of the European Marxist terrorist groups trained by the KGB and Stasi practiced very good surveillance tradecraft, but such sophisticated surveillance is the exception rather than the rule.

The term "tradecraft" is often used in describing a surveillance technique. Tradecraft is an espionage term that refers to techniques and procedures used in the field, but the term also implies that practicing these techniques and procedures effectively requires a bit of finesse. Tradecraft skills tend to be as much art as they are science, and surveillance tradecraft is no exception. As with any other art, the fundamentals can be taught, but it takes time and practice to become a skilled surveillance practitioner. Most individuals involved in terrorist planning simply do not devote the time necessary to master the art of surveillance, and because of this, they display terrible techniques, use sloppy procedures, and generally lack finesse when conducting surveillance.

The U.S. government trains counterintelligence officers using the TEDD method: (repeated observation of an individual over) time, (in different) environments, (over various) distances, and (with suspicious) demeanor. These four attributes help signal when you are the subject of a surveillance operation and can be picked up on through a comprehensive surveillance detection route.

2.1.5 Evolution of Surveillance Detection in Modern Times

In the wake of the U.S. embassy bombings in Kenya and Tanzania in 1998, Congress provided the State Department with $1.5 billion in emergency supplemental funding to strengthen security worldwide. Of this, $75 million went into a new and innovative surveillance detection program for 154 posts. The State Department has also made progress in implementing many of its planned security upgrades, including enhancing vehicle inspection and security guard programs, hiring additional special agents and other security staff, and instituting a new surveillance detection program designed to identify hostile surveillance activities and potential attackers. In 1998, the U.S. Department of State experienced approximately 150 attacks directly against U.S. embassies abroad; in 2002, following the stand-up of the surveillance detection program, there were 8 attacks directly on U.S embassies abroad. Coincidence?

Following the attacks of 9/11, the U.S. Pentagon hired contractors to provide a surveillance detection capability on and around the Pentagon Reservation until such time it could formulate and institute its own capability of surveillance operations specialists and stood up its own organic, robust surveillance detection capability. It has proven a successful antiterrorism tool for the iconic building.

Private sector corporations are discovering the value of a surveillance and threat detection program as well. Executive protection has recently grasped the concept as a covert means to personal protection that allows for the principal or protectee to have a protective detail that is innocuous. Unlike traditional security measures that react to threats, protective intelligence teams search proactively for evidence of hostile activity before an attack can be planned and launched. This allows the protective security team to keep on the positive side of the action/reaction equation and avoid potential problems. Certainly, protective intelligence efforts are complicated in a very busy urban environment, but a high level of activity on the street also complicates the operations of surveillance teams. Although countersurveillance teams are valuable, they cannot operate in a vacuum. They need to be part of a larger protective intelligence program that includes analytical and investigative functions. Investigations and analysis are two closely related yet distinct components that can help focus the countersurveillance operations on the most likely or most vulnerable targets, help analyze the observations of the countersurveillance team, and investigate any suspicious individuals observed.

High-value targets such as casinos, iconic buildings, and other fixed site facilities are beginning to embrace threat detection methodology as a means of preventing criminal and terrorist incidents, which ultimately favors lower insurance premiums. Therefore, the methodology is making the corporation money.

Critical infrastructure and key resources have recently developed a keen interest in utilizing threat detection in areas such as oil and gas industries, pipeline security, rail and port security, dams, bridges, and water systems to name just a few.

There are patent applications for surveillance detection systems and process techniques for automatically detecting when an individual is under surveillance. Big data algorithmic artificial intelligence software has exploded on the scene with its capabilities to recognize anomalous behaviors through closed-circuit television-activity. More on this can be found in Chapter 4: Conducting Surveillance Detection.

2.1.6 Surveillance Detection and the Law

There a great deal of issues surrounding the perception of the "surveillance state" in the United States and abroad. However, threat detection is the precursor of activity that is a simple observation of activities in and around a protected facility or terrorist target. Currently, there are no U.S. laws that prohibit surveillance and threat detection activity. With that said, jurisdictional issues exist for law enforcement that restrict where this activity can occur, and it is incumbent upon those law enforcement departments and agencies to operate within their defined jurisdictions. To that end, it is not the gathering of the information but how that gained information is utilized, stored, and collated for actionable intelligence that must comply with civil liberties and privacy protection acts.

As mentioned previously, studies by Smith and colleagues (1999) revealed that most terrorist incident preparation occurs approximately 3 months prior to attack and generally lasts between 12 days and 2 months. While some preparatory acts are not as overt as others, over three-quarters of preincident planning activity is overtly observable criminal behavior (Smith et al., 1999). It is important to note that the aforementioned studies also revealed that over 62% of terrorist groups conducted their last preparatory act on the day of the incident while another 9% conducted their last preparatory act just the day before (Smith et al., 1999). This alone is a good reason for first responders and police personnel to remain vigilant in order to attempt to detect any of the aforementioned methods of preincident planning by terrorist organizations.

Once these activities are detected, prosecutors and law enforcement personnel have a variety of legislative tools at their disposal to prevent terrorist incidents before they occur—the most obvious of which is the Patriot Act. Some of the fundamental system-wide provisions of the Patriot Act are covered in Sections 201, 203, 206, and 212. For example, Section 201 of the Patriot Act allows using currently existing wiretap, pen register, and dialed number recorder provisions to investigate offenses a given terrorist group or cell is likely to commit (U.S. Department of Justice, 2005).

Section 203 takes down the "wall" that used to inhibit information exchange between law enforcement and intelligence (U.S. Department of Justice, 2005). This relatively new free flow of information allows law enforcement to utilize intelligence agencies as sources of information regarding a particular terrorist group's motives. The U.S. Department of Justice (2005) has credited Section 203 as being an instrumental tool in facilitating the revocation of visas of suspected terrorists and has helped prevent re-entry of suspected terrorists into the United States. It has also enhanced greatly the ability of law enforcement to track sources of terrorist funding and identify terrorist operatives overseas.

Section 206 allows the Foreign Intelligence Surveillance Authority to authorize "roving surveillance," meaning that wiretaps can be attached to a particular person rather than a particular communication device (U.S. Department of Justice, 2005). This is a significant step forward, as previous laws did not account for changing technologies such as cordless telephones, cellular phones, and the Internet. For example, they only allowed very specific communication devices to be wiretapped, such as specific phone lines, specific phone numbers, or the base units of cordless phones but not the phones in and of themselves.

Finally, Section 212 allows providers of electronic communications to disclose customer records or the content of communications (e.g., phone records, e-mails, and the content of text messages) to government agencies in emergency situations involving "immediate danger of death or serious physical injury" (U.S. Department of Justice, 2005).

The aforementioned Patriot Act provisions are only a few of the many counterterrorism measures available to law enforcement. These measures improve law enforcement capabilities by allowing for enhanced ease in the development of probable cause, thereby allowing officers to take more immediate action in the disruption of preincident planning and the prevention of subsequent terror attacks.

Most federal law pertinent to terror investigation, prevention, and prosecution is contained within Title 18 of the U.S. Code. However, other titles of the federal code are available to law enforcement (especially federal and task force agents) in the fight against terrorism depending on their jurisdiction of legal code. Examples of non-Patriot Act federal law that apply to counterterrorism include the following.

Title 50 of the U.S. Code can also be utilized in the prosecution of terrorists for preincident planning as related to military installations. For example, 50 USC 795 makes it illegal to photograph or sketch U.S. Department of Defense installations (Cornell Law, n.d.). And 50 USC 797 makes it illegal to trespass on any U.S. military installation (Cornell Law, n.d.). In addition to relevant federal law, law enforcement officers should be familiar with their own state's laws pertaining to the prosecution of terrorism and terrorist acts as the implementation of state legislation to combat terrorism has become more common in the United States since 9/11.

Aside from direct violations of the aforementioned code sections, law enforcement should also remember the concept of arrests based on inchoate offenses, by which an offender can be charged for conspiracy, facilitation, solicitation, or even attempt to commit violations of the aforementioned or other laws. Based on this principle, simply planning a terrorist attack (meaning the implementation of any preincident tactic) is punishable by the same punitive measures used to prosecute the perpetrators of a completed attack.

While counterterrorism and terrorism prevention are concepts traditionally associated with our nation's intelligence agencies, there are many basic avenues law enforcement can take in fighting terrorism. Simply keeping an eye out for indicators of preincident planning is integral to counterterrorism efforts nationwide. Patriot Act provisions assist law enforcement efforts greatly by facilitating more efficient terrorist monitoring and probable cause development. Finally, familiarization with state and federal law pertaining to the prevention of terrorist attacks is an absolute must.

Terrorism presents a challenge to law enforcement as it requires police to act proactively against crimes (terrorist acts) that, in many cases, have not yet been committed. If the police wait, as they do traditionally, to react to terrorist crimes after they are committed, then the roles of the police are that of a first responder and an investigator. The public, however, expects police to deal with terrorism differently. This is mainly because crimes such as rape, theft, robbery, and even murder target the individual while terrorism targets the public. As such, the public demands that the police act to prevent terrorism before it becomes a criminal reality.

Police officers are given the rights to search and seizure based on probable cause (*Terry vs Ohio*) and to stop a person for inquiry based on reasonable suspicion. These rights were afforded to officers in order to help them prevent a crime that they believe is about to occur. To prove a crime, officers need to find evidence. However, when it comes to terrorism, evidence and weapons are not always there to find even at the execution of the attack. Let's consider 9/11 and assume for a minute that the terrorists would have been caught prior to boarding the planes.

Would we have had the foresight to articulate probable cause based on the terrorists' behavior and, if so, would we have regarded their box cutters as weapons (evidence) for a possible hijacking? Probably not.

In order to reach reasonable suspicion, officers must rely on their training and experience to come up "with an articulable and particularized belief that criminal activity is afoot" [*Orleans vs United States*, 517 U.S. 690 696 (1996) *Illinois vs Gates*, 462 U.S at 235]. To be able to articulate terrorism-related reasonable suspicion, officers must be trained and gain experience in terrorism methods of operations. In other words, officers must be able to look at a situation or activity (suspicion) and have the capability to explain what they are seeing through their terrorist eyes. Officers not trained (or not having the experience) in doing offensive surveillance, building a bomb or developing a terrorist plan among other things, will never be able to explain what they see as a terrorism-related reasonable cause.

As in the case of reasonable suspicion, to develop probable cause, officers need to fall back on their training and experience in order to describe "known facts and circumstances that are sufficient to warrant a man of reasonable prudence in the belief that contraband or evidence of a crime will be found" [*Orleans vs United States*, 517 U.S. 690 696 (1996) *Illinois vs Gates*, 462 U.S. at 213,238 (1983)]. Finding bombs and terrorist weapons is a difficult task, as almost anything can be used as a weapon and bombs appear in countless shapes and forms. In order to develop a terrorist-related probable cause, officers need to rely more on information provided by the suspect than on tangible evidence. To obtain this information, officers must utilize different questioning techniques then those used when interviewing suspected criminals.

Approaching the suspect from a "law enforcement" angle will probably not work because the suspect has yet to have broken the law in the case of identifiable reasonable suspicion and probable cause. Moreover, cooperation and information are needed to establish probable cause or refute the reasonable suspicions found. Asking for an ID and checking the suspect's criminal record are unlikely to help the officer because most terrorists avoid criminal activities and their records are therefore clean. The key to success lies in open-ended, public service-oriented and inquisitive questioning geared toward refuting reasonable suspicions. In essence, the questioning that the officer conducts should resemble that of a receptionist asking politely about the intentions of a visitor entering a building and not that of an officer who has just pulled over a person for speeding recklessly on the highway.

Using nonthreatening, public service-oriented questioning allows law enforcement to

1. Refute reasonable suspicions
2. Develop probable cause, as reasonable suspicions were not refuted
3. Deter the terrorist or arrest him/her
4. Provide the innocent with a great public service
5. Avoid liability and law suits

Finally, reasonable suspicion and probable cause are tools given to police to enforce the law even when the law has not yet been broken. Bearing this in mind, police must realize that in dealing with terrorism, prevention always supersedes enforcement and the ultimate goal behind terrorism-related reasonable suspicion and probable cause is to give police the legal justification to intervene, deter, and prevent— not necessarily to arrest and convict.

2.2 The Terrorist Attack Cycle

The key to mitigating and preventing terrorist and criminal attacks is to understand the terrorist attack cycle, which is composed of

- Terrorist Preattack and Attack Methodology
- Indicators of Preattack Operations: TTP— Tactics, Techniques, and Procedures

As discussed, the challenge for security officers is to sift through the bustle and commotion of their surroundings and select those clues that pinpoint a threat—*to find the needle in the haystack*. It may seem like an impossible task; however, to plan their attack, the terrorist must surface from that haystack.

We know that every successful terrorist attack has been preceded by extensive surveillance, reconnaissance, and logistical activity.

When criminals want to break into your house, what do they do? They case the joint. In other words, because terrorists and criminals telegraph what they intend to do, we have to become security-savvy enough to recognize when this happens.

This is the terrorist's greatest vulnerability.

To gather information for the attack, the terrorist must present himself, and he will create patterns of suspicious behavior.

To exploit this vulnerability, we must become intimately familiar with the terrorists' **TTPs**. And just as we study the terrorists' TTPs, they study ours and adjust theirs accordingly to avoid detection and thwart our security measures.

We can identify the terrorists' TTPs by detecting patterns of behavior indicative of preattack surveillance if we adopt a surveillance program that will

- Identify
- Document
- Collate
- Analyze
- Share

Identify. First and foremost, we must identify patterns of behavior as suspicious activity.

What is suspicious activity? Use this simple test to determine suspicious activity: what is normal vs not normal?

Observe your surroundings. What are the typical behaviors of people visiting or traveling by your facility? If it's a hot summer day, would it be "normal or not normal" for a customer to wear a heavy coat? Would it be "normal or not normal" for a woman to spend hours outside your entrance on a freezing winter day with a baby carriage? How about a random tourist asking questions about your shift change or a car that keeps parking in a loading zone but never takes a passenger? The purchase of unusually large amounts of chemicals? Someone searching through your trash bins? Timing how long it takes your vehicle barriers to lower and raise? Pacing your perimeter? Taking clandestine photographs of your employee entrance?

If you see something suspicious—*not normal*—you report that to your security officers.

The campaign "If You See Something, Say Something" is an effective program used to raise public awareness of "not normal" terrorist-related behavior and to report that suspicious activity.

Next we connect the dots.

Document. Now that we've defined what suspicious behavior is, we must document that information to initiate the suspicious activity reporting (SAR) process. That process begins when security officers collect reports from guards, employees, and the public about "not normal" incidents.

The reports serve to encapsulate suspicious behavior to provide information for statistical analysis and to help understand the meaning of suspicious behavior against the backdrop of "normal" activity. These reports must record information in a thorough and comprehensive manner and in a way that facilitates retrieving details about the incidents. A standardized format for a written report will help ensure that adequate details about the incident are recorded. These details may not appear relevant at the time, but may help illuminate a pattern in the suspicious behavior. For example, noting the weather conditions may seem like a trivial detail but it may point out that the person conducting suspicious behavior was overdressed for the local climate and could be hiding cameras underneath his or her clothing.

While a standardized reporting procedure will help document suspicious behavior, such a procedure must not be so rigid that it would preclude the documentation of information that would give a more complete understanding of the suspicious activity. Remember, because terrorists and criminals are always adjusting their TTPs to circumvent our surveillance detection, relying on a checklist of suspicious behavior may miss a new pattern of suspicious activity. Additionally, you should have a way of documenting photography and video that also captured "not normal" behavior.

At this point privacy concerns must be mentioned. Your surveillance detection program must include a well-defined privacy policy that provides guidelines addressing privacy matters such as the documentation and retention of personally identifying characteristics and how that information is distributed within your organization and with other entities (such as law enforcement).

Collate. We must next gather our reports and note their information on spreadsheets and/or Gantt or flowcharts with an eye on how this information reaches your facility's chief of security. This phase of the SAR process should also address the retention of reports (and associated photography, video, etc.) for later use and in a manner that cultivates a robust institutional memory. Such an institutional memory is needed to maintain an effective surveillance detection program in case of changes in security personnel.

Characterization of suspicious behavior should correspond with the information provided in the narrative descriptive of your reports. This would include details about how and why the behavior provoked suspicion. This will help your facility's chief of security sift through suspicious behavior to determine a pattern of suspicious activity and see if there are larger issues behind this activity: Perhaps the same person has been seen making videos at different buildings on your facility?

Analyze. At this phase of the SAR process, you must analyze information to determine the extent of suspicious behavior and see whether there are links to a credible threat. This analysis should be driven by both a risk-assessment survey that has pinpointed your vulnerabilities and a decision-making framework that guides and directs your surveillance detection efforts. This framework should be a comprehensive review of suspicious behavior—with a willingness to look further into the issue—versus using a checklist that relies simply on an enumerated "not normal" behavior. The tendency is to gather all information about every activity, which would swamp your analysis with extraneous details. Instead, your surveillance detection analysis should focus on behavioral-based indicators. These indicators can be classified to determine if a pattern of suspicious activity is developing. Once a pattern has been identified, then you can see if it illuminates a threat to your facility since you should be aware of your risks and vulnerabilities. Included in this analysis should be a decision to "share or not share" information about suspicious activity.

Share. Now to the next phase of the SAR process. At this point, we have identified suspicious activity and have decided to share that information. But with whom? And why?

Government facilities should already belong to a security administration network with established lines of communication. Typically, these lines of communication feed into local law enforcement, who in turn forward information to the regional Joint Terrorism Task Force (JTTF). Local law enforcement should reach out to private entities, such as banks, and public institutions, such as universities or mass transit, to establish channels for the uptake and dissemination of suspicious activity. All levels of awareness—from the cash register clerk at the corner beauty supply to the construction site manager to the beat cop—should know who to report suspicious activity to. Sharing the information can be as simple as making a phone call to the local sheriff or through a more sophisticated process that collects reports over the Internet.

As to the why, law enforcement and the JTTF will gather reports about suspicious activity and analyze this information to determine if a credible threat exists. Additionally, law enforcement and the JTTF can bring resources to investigate in greater detail suspicious activity and decide the extent of the threat.

eGuardian is the primary U.S. government program used to share SAR information. The FBI instituted the eGuardian program to streamline the sharing of terrorist-related activities across federal, state, tribal, and local jurisdictions. However, access to eGuardian is limited to law enforcement and defense agencies and is considered a one-way pipeline of information flow. Meaning, information goes up the pipe to the FBI and the national JTTF and seldom comes back down to you.

Other means of sharing information include commercial products such as TrapWire. These products allow you to enter SAR information and, in turn, see similar reports submitted by facilities within your network. This shared information can be useful in analyzing locally reported suspicious behavior to determine if a pattern of suspicious activity does exist.

Who conducts surveillance against us? Who are the bad guys?

- *Terrorist groups (professional, state sponsored)*. These groups are organized, trained, equipped, and funded by state governments or by an organization with an infrastructure that can provide adequate resources to field terrorists. These groups have a formal structured hierarchy and can be surprisingly bureaucratic in the management of their operations. Their actions serve to support the political agenda of their sponsor. Members draw pay and are directed by higher ups in the organization. An example of a professional terrorist group would be al Qaeda or the Irish Republican Army; a state-sponsored group would be Hezbollah, which receives funding, training, and equipment from Iran.

- *Terrorists (amateurs, wannabes, "lone wolves").* These terrorists are not affiliated directly with a professional or a state-sponsored terrorist group, but take it upon themselves to execute attacks in the name of the professional or state group. These individuals usually receive little training and only enough support (such as firearms and explosives) to conduct their independent operations. Frequently, such individuals are recruited for martyrdom (suicide) assignments and are thus considered expendable proxies by their professional or state patrons. The terrorists who conducted the 2008 Mumbai attacks are one example.

- *Foreign intelligence services.* Agents from a foreign intelligence service will attempt to gather information to further their government's agendas, often to gain a military or political advantage. These agents are well trained in espionage and supported by an extensive intelligence-gathering base. They will use more subtle and sophisticated techniques to gather information. China and Pakistan are two governments that field agents against the United States.

- *Insurgents/anarchists (military extremists, sovereign citizens, militia).* These terrorists execute attacks in support of their single-issue extremist agendas and include individuals and groups that use violence to promote an antitax agenda, declare themselves independent of any government or civil authority, support acts promoting an environmental cause, or protest abortion, etc. These groups are self-funded and self-trained and difficult to stop until they perpetrate acts of violence. Examples include the Utah Free Militia (sovereign citizens), the Unabomber Ted Kaczynski (anarchist), Earth Liberation Front (vandalism and arson committed in the name of protecting the environment), and the Olympic bomber Eric Rudolf (antiabortion).

- *Violent protesters.* These groups use the cover of legitimate protest to disrupt the activities of government and business in support of a mainly anarchist agenda. Violent protestors can employ very sophisticated and imaginative tactics to draw media attention, such as taking over a bank and turning it into a homeless shelter. They often seek to provoke a violent confrontation between peaceful protestors and the police. Violent protest groups are generally amorphous organizations that lack a defined leadership structure and yet are well educated in countersurveillance techniques. Black Bloc is one such group.
- *Criminals.* Unlike other terrorists, criminals are motivated solely by the need for monetary gain rather than to serve a political or military agenda. Frequently, criminals take advantage of targets of opportunity and so compress their surveillance and attack cycle. A mugger is one example. Their methodology centers on not getting caught. However, in some instances, criminals may execute well-planned and rehearsed attacks such as to rob a bank or an armored car, smuggle large quantities of drugs, or to murder rivals.

2.2.1 Preattack and Attack Methodology

This is how terrorists and criminals work.

The terrorist surveillance team conducts its preattack and attack operations according to the following **surveillant mission objectives.**

- *Surveil and collect intelligence ("collect every piece and scrap of information").* Terrorists use all possible means to record as much information as possible on intended targets. Video and photography are especially preferred because they can be used multiple times. The intelligence is often documented and submitted in professional formats and presentations. The reports are very detailed and prepared in formats resembling an academic thesis or business briefing with the intention of providing upper levels with the full scope of information to help them plan, direct, and execute an attack. Additionally, the reports are an opportunity for the surveillant to impress his superiors with his competence and potential.
- *Report to the boss (the upper levels— command and leadership).* What the surveillance team does not want to be told is that they didn't get enough intelligence. Surveillant reports should provide enough information for the upper levels to proceed to the next step in their preattack planning. Furthermore, surveillants will ensure that the reports are as complete as possible to reduce the need for follow-up reports and extraneous communication that could jeopardize operational security.

- *Train the attack team.* The purpose of surveillance is to train the attack team. The more detailed the intelligence, the greater the chance for a successful attack. The surveillance team will have first-hand knowledge of the target and are the individuals to best provide information necessary for the attack. Videos are particularly useful in walking the attack team through its preparations.
- *Do not get caught.* Expect surveillants to practice extreme measures to ensure operation security. They will use cover stories to justify their interest in targets. Terrorists will study our TTPs to work around our security measures and avoid detection. An attack is executed not only by those who attack the target physically but also by those surveillants who gathered intelligence, identified vulnerabilities, and trained the attack team. Surveillants strive to escape and perform more missions in support of their organization's agenda.

Terrorists recognize the need to appear unobtrusive and to help them blend in with the local populace, especially in the United States. al-Qa'ida publishes the magazine *Inspire*, a slick, English-language, how-to-guide for terrorists (Figure 2.1). The magazine, offered in both paper and online versions, offers tips on local customs, dress, and dialect.

Inspire is aimed at the amateur and wanna-be terrorist not trained to the level of professional and state-sponsored terrorists. The magazine seeks to further indoctrinate and provide basic information to help inexperienced terrorists conduct attacks. Most surveillants are not very

Figure 2.1 "Don't stick out like a sore thumb."

sophisticated and their lack of awareness aids our surveillance detection efforts if we are vigilant regarding "normal vs not normal."

Additional guidance on how to blend in can be provided by individuals or organizations sympathetic to the terrorist's cause. For example, an expatriate religious leader or staff from a neighborhood school could give tips to a terrorist on what the locals wear.

2.2.1.1 The Preattack and Attack Methodology Process (Figure 2.2)

- **Receive initial list of targets.** The upper level of a terrorist organization develops an initial list of targets, perhaps as many as 15—an attack on which would further its goals. A terrorist group would select targets of high political value, while criminals would seek targets of high monetary value. Depending on the group's agenda, the targets could be

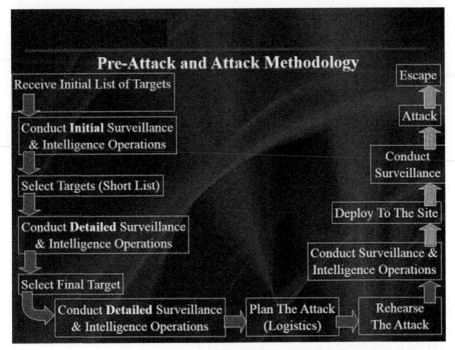

Figure 2.2 The preattack and attack methodology process.

military, financial, or industrial facilities; government buildings; or individuals to be assassinated. An attack on these targets could either cause serious military and economic damage or their destruction could be of symbolic importance.

- For example: Our terrorists have decided to mount an attack on a major American city with the aim of punishing the United States for its perceived anti-Islamic policies. They select New York and dispatch a surveillance team to gather information on possible targets to include Times Square, Wall Street, the Statue of Liberty, the Empire State Building, and the subway system.

- **Conduct initial surveillance and intelligence operations.** The upper level dispatches small teams to cursory surveil all the targets on this initial list. The primary goals of this initial surveillance are to determine if an attack on any of these targets meet the organization's goals and to define if the target as a "hard" or "soft" target. By "hard" or "soft," we mean vulnerable to attack. A possible target may be a fortified building but lax security and easy access would define the building as a "soft" target. Conversely, a bank may seem vulnerable but an extensive alarm system and an alert security force would define the bank as a "hard" target. The surveillants will gather information to report, such as the orientation of the target; adjacent roads, parking lots, public transportation, and proximity to other businesses; employee traffic; and obvious security precautions, such as guards and outside cameras.

- Continuing with our example: The upper level selects two individuals to comprise the surveillance team. They will gather information about the New York targets and note both vulnerabilities and if an attack would address the group's agenda.

- **Select targets.** The surveillance team submits their reports to the upper level who review the initial list reports. Terrorists and criminals will defer to "soft" targets as these assure chances of success. The upper level analyzes and decides which of these targets best serves its goals. They narrow the short list to perhaps three targets.

  - Our example: The upper level decides that an attack on Wall Street would not cause sufficient damage considering the logistics needed to mount an effective attack. The Statue of Liberty is guarded too closely and difficult to destroy. After culling through the rest of the list, the upper level settles on Times Square, the Empire State Building, and the Metro subway system as the "softest" targets.

- **Conduct detailed surveillance and intelligence operations.** The surveillance team conducts new surveillance of the short-listed targets and produces more detailed reports. Some examples of this more detailed information could be how many employees; how many windows in the target building; how thick are the doors; which way are the security cameras pointed; what is the critical infrastructure supporting this building; how far away is the police department; what about the internal structure of the facility; what are the security arrangements for access; where are the evacuation routes; what are the best times for inflicting mass casualties? At this point in their preattack planning the terrorists will be among you.

  - Our example: The surveillance team returns to the targets on their short list to prepare a more detailed report. They collect more thorough intelligence on the vulnerabilities and the suitability of the targets. The surveillants will look at the timing of the possible attack to maximize damage and will scrutinize security precautions.

- **Select final target.** The surveillance team transmits these reports to their upper levels. They review the reports and cull the list down to a final target by deciding what is the softest target—with the greatest assurance of success.

  - Our example: The upper level studies the reports to select a final target. They cross off the Empire State Building because detailed surveillance revealed that security precautions would prevent the emplacement of explosives sufficient to topple the structure. Likewise, an attack on Times Square during the New Year's celebration would require too much logistics for a comprehensive coordinated attack. The upper level decides on the New York City Metro subway system.

- **Conduct detailed surveillance and intelligence operations.** The surveillance team deploys back to the final target to gather the necessary intelligence to execute the attack (and escape). Now the team collects very detailed information about the target, such as mapping the facility; how comprehensive is the security camera coverage; what are the emergency response procedures; in case of an evacuation, where do the workers gather?
  - Our example: The terrorists will maintain surveillance on the subway system to make sure nothing has changed that could affect the attack. Additionally, the surveillance will look for clues, such as heightened security, that could reveal if the attack has been compromised. As attack planning proceeds, the surveillants need to know the security arrangements protecting the New York City subway system. Who provides security? Are there metal or explosive detectors? Will there be countersurveillance? When do people arrive? By what means and from what direction? Where are the surveillance cameras? Would it be possible to position explosive devices within the subway? How vulnerable are the passengers to an attack by

gunfire? Would it be feasible to use smaller explosive devices to force people out of the subway and close to vehicle-born improvised explosive devices (VBIEDs) planted outside?

- **Plan the attack** (logistics). The upper level determines the type of attack. This planning would include the composition of the attack team. In the case of a "lone-wolf" terrorist, the attack team would most likely be one individual. For attacks by state-sponsored terrorist groups, the upper level will decide on the size and number of attack teams based on the amount of damage desired to be inflicted and the logistics available. The priority concern by the upper level is causing the highest possible body count. In the execution of the attack, what is going to draw unwanted attention to the attack team? Will the attack require one team of three individuals or will the three attack independently? Would two teams of more individuals be more effective? What type and size of weapons (explosives, guns)? Best method of attack: backpacks, suitcases, or VBIEDs; chemical or biological? Will the bombs be left unattended? How will they be detonated?
  - Our example: Based on experience, terrorists will most likely use triacetone triperoxide, peroxyacetone (TATP) as the explosive for an attack on the New York City Metro subway. This powerful, yet unstable, explosive is a favorite of terrorists because it can be made easily with household ingredients and is difficult to detect. TATP was used in the July 7, 2005 London bombings. al-Qa'ida's *Inspire* magazine shows how

to make and preserve TATP. The three most likely types of attack on the subway would be (1) the use of combined arms, meaning gunmen using automatic weapons and grenades; (2) a "drop-and-pop," which is a IED left behind such as an unattended backpack or a bomb dropped in a trash can and either command or detonated remotely; (3) or a suicide attack (martyrdom). The upper level could also decide on a more sophisticated attack, using smaller explosives to channel passengers through evacuation routes and then detonating larger VBIEDs outside to target both escaping passengers and first responders as they're gathered together. In our example, the upper level has chosen three terrorists for a suicide attack using backpack bombs for the team to arrive together and then ride separate subway cars.

- **Rehearse the attack.** The surveillance team rehearses the attack with dry runs that could include driving vehicles along the attack route (studying the local road conditions, counting the traffic lights), testing signaling procedures, walking along the building to confirm security measures, and observing the response to building evacuations. The surveillance team will select the best times for the attack and will travel the planned route using the same means planned for the attack team, be it on foot, using cabs, mass transit, etc. The surveillance team will note if and what fares are needed and if the attack team will need to change busses or trains. They will also time the travel needed to deploy from the staging area to the attack objective. The surveillance team will rehearse the attack within a half-hour window of the planned attack time. The goal of rehearsal is for the attack team to deploy in "cruise control," where they have all the directions and means (such as transit fare) to reach their objective without having to think about anything but executing the attack. The number of dry runs varies with the complexity of the attack. Two or three rehearsals may be sufficient for complex attacks. However, prior to the Oklahoma City bombing, Timothy McVeigh simply drove through the building's parking lot and, based on his observation, decided where to park his explosive-laden rental truck. In the case of the 2005 London bombings, the terrorists performed five to six dry runs in the 2 weeks prior to the attack.

- Our example: Based on their previous surveillance, the surveillance team has confirmed that early-morning rush hour is the best time to inflict maximum casualties on the New York City subway and will perform dry runs in the 7:30 to 8:30 AM window. Eighty-nine percent of terrorist attacks have occurred between 7:00 and 8:00 AM. The surveillance team needs to know exactly where the three individuals of the attack team will be during the attack.

- **Conduct surveillance and intelligence operations.** Now that the logistics are in place and the rehearsals completed, the surveillance team continues to monitor the target to ensure that nothing has changed at the objective that could affect the attack. This surveillance will be conducted on at least the day of the attack but may be as soon as 3 days prior. The surveillance team's function is to only observe.

- Our example: The surveillance team watches the subway stop designated for use by the attack team. The surveillance team wants to make sure that nothing unexpected has presented itself, such as a police K9 unit or portable explosive detectors.

- **Deploy to the site.** The surveillance team issues the order for the attack to proceed. The attack team deploys to the site and the necessary logistics (vehicles, explosives, guns, etc.,) are in place. At this point, the attack will be difficult to stop by security.

  - Our example: On time and undetected, the attack team enters the subway system with their backpacks. They buy the appropriate Metro tickets and board their designated cars.

- **Conduct surveillance.** The surveillance team continues to monitor the target as the attack team moves into position and then gives the signal to execute the final stages of the attack. The surveillance team is most likely in cell phone contact with the attack team to call off the mission in the event it may fail. The disruption could be from the unexpected closure of the stop because of an unrelated accident or from the police conducting random checks.

  - Our example: The surveillance team is in place, with one individual outside the Metro stop and another inside by the turnstiles. Both surveillants give the "go" signal for the attack to proceed.

- **Attack.** The surveillance team observes the attack and reports results to upper levels.

The surveillance team frequently videos an attack for postattack analysis and for use in propaganda. This is a common practice in Afghanistan during an IED attack. These videos are broadcast to demonstrate the vulnerability of the United States against the might of the terrorists.

- At this point, only a miracle can prevent the attack. The terrorists have managed to thwart defensive measures and are inside your protected area. This reality stresses the importance of surveillance and threat detection.
  - Our example: The surveillance team observes the attack from a safe area outside the Metro subway station. They use this opportunity to judge the effectiveness of the attack and to observe the reaction by both the casualties and the first responders.
- **Escape.** The surveillance team escapes to avoid capture and to contribute to further missions: *Live to fight another day.* The terrorists understand that their war is not a one-time shot and their cause will require more attacks. The surveillance team is an invaluable asset to the upper level and is not an expendable resource such as a suicide bomber. The surveillance team represents the "eyes and ears" in hostile territory and are intimately familiar with their enemies' patterns of behavior and TTPs. Focused and often highly educated, the surveillance team leader is the ground commander and understands attack operations, surveillance, and how to collect and report intelligence.
  - Our example: One member of the surveillance team travels by bus away from New York City to another city to return home

and debrief the upper level personally. The other member of the surveillance team remains in New York to collect more post-attack intelligence and to surveil additional attack objectives.

When the terrorist attack methodology is reviewed, we see that at numerous times in this process the terrorist must make himself present at the target to conduct surveillance and intelligence operations and rehearse the attack.

This is the terrorists' greatest vulnerability: when they must present themselves to gather information for the attack. *This is when we can stop them!*

Terrorists do not pick a target arbitrarily to attack. Now that we understand their methodology, what does their surveillance process look like? We need to know that terrorists (and criminals) will:

- **Conduct detailed preattack surveillance and intelligence collection of their target—reviewed earlier.**
- **Surveil you with a small team, generally composed of one to three individuals.** The "bad guys" seldom have the resources to deploy more surveillants and prefer to rely on a few trusted and trained individuals.
- **Surveil you over and over again to understand your patterns.** Terrorists are crafty and will vary their surveillance to gain a comprehensive understanding of your pattern of life. For example, if the terrorists have decided to attack an individual, on Monday, Wednesdays, and Fridays, they would surveil

the target's home to learn his schedule and movements. They would learn the target's daily routes. On Tuesday and Thursday, the surveillants would move farther along the routes to get more information and more details about the target's pattern of life. The terrorists may surveil you over a period of weeks, months, and even years.

- **Surveil you on-ground, in and around your facility, and in your face.** During the surveillance and intelligence phases, the terrorists must come in close proximity to you. They must expose themselves to observe and record you and your activities. The surveillants will be on foot, watching from taxis, observing from nearby balconies, and approaching to query your guards and employees. The surveillants will have to engage you directly, and it is at this time when they are vulnerable for detection.

- **Probe your security and test your reactions.** The surveillants need to know your security posture and state of vigilance. If possible, they will enter your facility to see how close they can approach their attack objective. They will use a ruse, such as delivering a pizza, or may learn what distracts the security detail, such as watching sports playoffs, and use that opportunity to sneak inside the facility. They will leave backpacks and suitcases behind and watch to see how much time it will take for the public and law enforcement to react to "unattended packages." On the flip side, this is the time when security can best detect suspicious behavior. For example, security officers may report that the same individual has been trying to get into their facility at various times or security videos may record that the same group of people has been leaving unattended backpacks on public transit.

- **Produce patterns of behavior that create suspicious activity.** The surveillants will question your security officers. Taken individually, these questions may seem innocuous, but when reviewed in total, they could reveal an unusual and suspicious interest in your facility. Also, the same individual may be stopping at your security gates and asking directions repeatedly or walking close to a secure facility and taking photos.

You exploit that vulnerability by observing and reporting their suspicious activity. *Remember: normal vs not normal.*

Just as the terrorists are trying to understand your pattern of life, you must also understand what the pattern around you is. What is "normal" in your environment? What is "normal" behavior? What are "normal" activities? Your best defense against the "bad guys" is to realize that "not normal" behavior is exhibited when they are presenting themselves.

2.2.2 Exploitation of the Terrorist Methodology

Now that we understand the terrorist preattack and attack methodology, this gives us an opportunity for a *paradigm shift*, to turn the tables on the bad guys, to go from *reactive to proactive* and stop them during their preattack operations.

To do so, we must recognize the terrorists' tactics, techniques, and procedures—indicators of preattack operations—which are

- Who?
- What?
- When?
- Where?
- How?

2.2.2.1 Who *Are They Going to Surveil and Collect Intelligence On?*

Terrorists and criminals choose high-value targets (HVTs) that support their goals and achieve "the most bang for their buck." The upper level of a terrorist organization will select targets that are of significant military or political value and to effect political change. Attacks against the United States are conducted to express resentment against American dominance. For example, if state-sponsored terrorists were interested in the economic collapse of the United States, they would attack Wall Street and the New York Stock Exchange. However, sovereign citizens would attack a federal building to demonstrate their resentment to civil authority and encourage public resistance against the government. A lone-wolf terrorist may attack on behalf of his perceived duty to jihad and in the name of a terrorist organization. Criminals will select targets that promote their criminal enterprise, usually large quantities of cash or commodities of high monetary value.

An initial target list would include HVTs such as

- *Embassies.* These could be foreign embassies on U.S. soil that support causes contrary to the goals of the terrorists or American embassies abroad.

- *Vital economic centers.* Banking and financial institutions (Prudential Financial Center, New York Stock Exchange, Citigroup headquarters, IMF, World Bank) as these represent the dominance of U.S. commerce and the American dollar.
- *Government facilities.* The White House would be targeted because it is perceived as an iconic symbol of U.S. political power.
- *Military installations.* For example, Ft. Dix was selected as a target for jihad because it represented U.S. military dominance and the suppression of their Islamic brothers and sisters.
- *Refineries and nuclear power plants.* An attack to such facilities would cause severe economic hardship.
- *Bridges and dams.* The destruction of these structures would cause much social disruption and economic distress.
- *Highly populated attractions (stadiums, amusement parks, religious centers, shopping malls).* These institutions represent soft targets with enormous economic and propaganda value.
- *High-density modes of transportation (airports, subways, bus terminals).* An attack would cause many casualties and disrupt transportation with a disastrous economic affect.
- *Important cultural landmarks (the Statue of Liberty).* An attack would represent a significant blow against an iconic national treasure.
- *Places of immorality and sin (cruise ships, casinos).* These institutions offend the beliefs of the pious terrorists and represent the destructive forces of the infidel's way of life.

- *Persons to assassinate (political and military personnel, foreign tourists).* Terrorists will target individuals to effect political change or to send a message—that the terrorists are capable of retribution. Political assassinations are preceded by significant amounts of detailed surveillance. If average citizens are assassinated, it is because they were targets of opportunity.
- *Prisons in order to free captured "brothers."* The freeing of their brothers is just as important as an attack on American citizens.

2.2.2.2 What *Are They Going to Surveil and Collect Intelligence On?*

Once the terrorist upper level has selected an initial target list, surveillance teams are deployed to gather intelligence; this information would include

- Orientation of target
- Surveillance objectives
- Local streets and businesses
- Local traffic grid
- Parking lots
- Video cameras
- Perimeter security (guards, fencing, Jersey barriers, bollards)
- Location and number of employee entrances

The initial surveillance report is submitted to the upper level, who reviews the intelligence and creates a short list of targets. The surveillance team returns to the targets on the short list for a more detailed surveillance of

- Perimeter breach points.
- Which way the cameras are pointed.

- How thick is the front door?
- How many windows? Are they bulletproof glass?
- Power grid.
- Badges worn by employees.
- Collect dossiers on individual security guards (with as much personal information as possible: names, wives' names, types of car owned, favorite sports teams).
- How is the building constructed?
- Get inside the building.
- What about the structural beams inside the building?
- Who is in the building? At what times?
- How far away is the police department? The fire department?
- What is the response time? How many police will respond?
- Is there a childcare facility? When does it open? When does it close?
- Avenues of attack and escape.

The more detailed the intelligence sought by terrorists, the closer they must approach you and their target. They may even try to enter your facility. This will give you the opportunity to better detect and recognize "not normal" behavior.

2.2.2.3 When *Are They Going to Surveil and Collect Intelligence?*

Expect terrorists to surveil you *anytime* and *all the time*. Terrorists will approach your facility during "down" times—in the evenings, weekends, and holidays—to take advantage of relaxed vigilance. They will approach during hours of peak activity to blend in with the masses and to gauge the level of traffic. Terrorists will use this information in their target planning. Perhaps the best time to inflict mass casualties at a facility is when employees queue for entry outside the security perimeter. Terrorists will approach during visits by high-profile persons—politicians, business and military leaders, or celebrities—to study your security measures.

Terrorists will appear at their targets as noted in the preattack and attack methodology, which occur during the following.

- *Surveillance of initial list of targets.* This is when terrorists will initially surveil to gather intelligence for their upper levels to determine the best target for an attack. This surveillance is to gather a broad scope understanding of the targets.
- *Surveillance of short list of targets.* Terrorists will revisit your facility to gather more intelligence to refine their target list. They will perform extended observation and use photography and videos to record intelligence.
- *Detailed surveillance of final target.* The upper level of the terrorist organization has chosen your facility as their attack target. The surveillance team will gather extremely detailed intelligence for the attack team. They will attempt to enter your facility and approach your security officers to gather information through querying. Expect them to probe your security perimeter.
- *During the rehearsal.* The surveillance team will reconfirm its intelligence and make sure there are no changes at the facility that could jeopardize the attack. These changes could include a more comprehensive security force, closures of roads, or restricted access. The

attack team will use that intelligence to execute dry runs. At this point, the terrorists are at their most vulnerable because they will be in close proximity to your facility, and they will be in greater numbers (surveillance and attack teams). Plus they will be going through the motions of the attack—exhibiting patterns of suspicious behavior. For example, the attack may be carrying large backpacks stuffed with innocuous material to simulate actual explosives. Additionally, we can expect the terrorists, especially the attack team, to exhibit nervousness, anxiousness, and acute concern because, with the exceptions of state-sponsored terrorists, these individuals will not be well trained. They will probably be talking quite a bit with one another to relieve their stress and reassure themselves.

• *Before and during the attack.* The surveillance team will monitor the target and be pre-pared to issue the attack order. During the attack, the surveillance team will gather intel-ligence to determine the effectiveness of the attack.

Despite all the preparation by the terrorists, security personal can still thwart an attack by maintaining vigilance. However, once the attack is executed, the security officers will assume duties as dictated in their disaster preparation plans to treat casualties and contain damage. Even in this case, security officers should remain aware for "not normal" behavior. Perhaps there is an individual who doesn't flee like the others, and this person lingers to make a video. The surveillants will remain close by to record the attack to use in future training and to exploit its propaganda value.

2.2.2.4 Where *Are They Going to Surveil Us From?*

They will surveil you on-ground, in and around your facility, and up close—*in your face...literally!* Terrorists will approach you directly to query how long you have worked at this location, what time do the doors unlock, do you need a badge to get in, anddo you need to swipe the badge? They will get close enough to photograph your uniforms and employee badges. They will get wherever they need to be to understand your patterns and watch your reaction to their surveillance.

Terrorists will establish a **surveillance zone**—an area from which they can surveil you and the target adequately. A typical surveillance zone may exist in high rises that overlook your facility or it could be a parking lot outside your main entrance. In any case, once you identify a surveillance zone, it may be easier to pinpoint "not normal" behavior. For example, a car parked in a lot across the street may not be suspicious, that is, until you noticed the driver taking photos of your building covertly, with the driver never exiting the vehicle or picking up a passenger.

2.2.2.5 How *Are They Going to Surveil Us?*

There are eight distinctive suspicious "not normal" activities that reveal terrorist surveillance intent. It is important that security officers know to report these activities and that there is a mechanism to capture and document this information in a SAR process. These are the eight suspicious "not normal" activities.

1. Watching (Figure 2.3)
   - Loitering for no apparent reason or standing close to a sensitive area. Showing

Figure 2.3 Watching.

nervous behavior (exaggerated movements to relieve stress, looking behind to see of anyone is watching them).

- Target focus and fixation (tunnel vision). An individual may show an unusual interest in a particular aspect of your facility. For example, why would someone be focused on the guards around your entrance door?
- If mobile:
  - A car is usually an ideal platform for anonymous surveillance. How often do people take photographs from a car?
  - Lapping (especially sensitive areas). An individual may circle or walk back and forth across a facility to gather intelligence. Why would someone continue to walk pass a particular gate?
  - Route reversal. A person reverses course as a technique to ascertain if

he or she is being followed (i.e., shadowed or tailed). Such behavior should be considered "tradecraft."

Tradecraft is one set of TTPs used in espionage and clandestine surveillance. Of interest here are those tactics and techniques a terrorist would use to confirm being the subject of countersurveillance. The terrorist will use TTPs such as route reversal, hiding around a blind corner to surprise a tail, or moving to an "overwatch" position to identify any possible followers. Security officers need to be trained in tradecraft TTPs to avoid compromising their countersurveillance. The use of tradecraft is "not normal" behavior and identifies an individual as a trained surveillance operative.

2. Videotaping/photographing
   - Not "normal" subjects (trust your gut). Someone photographing the high-voltage lines into your building is "not normal."
   - Sensitive areas, for example, entrances into high-security buildings or delivery doors for money and high-dollar items.
   - May use accomplice to either help hide covert techniques or act as a decoy.
   - May use covert techniques such as a remote trigger to operate a camera from a slung position.
   - Panoramic shooting (of not "normal" areas). "It is preferable to photograph the area as a whole first, then the street of the desired location. If possible, panoramic pictures should be taken" (al Qaeda).
   - Terrorists will use video to record as much information as possible.

3. Writing/sketching
   - Note taking, texting, drawing, etc.
   - Showing an interest of sensitive areas.

- May watch and then sketch in another area. A person may linger outside an area to memorize details and then move to another area to sketch the details while still fresh.
- May use covert techniques (hide note pad).

4. Querying
   - Asking "not normal" questions:
     - "How many armed officers are on shift?"
     - "What are your shift change times?" (Shift change is a favorite time for targeting because guards can become complacent and get distracted.)
     - "How do you control that barrier?"
     - "Do you have access to rifles?"
   - Asking for "not normal" things.
     - "Please send me a copy of your blueprints."

5. Probing/testing security
   - Security measures:
     - Perimeter protection. Where are the breach points? Test reaction to an intrusion.
     - Vehicle barriers/bollards. Is there a substantial gap between them? Are they robust enough to stop a car? A truck?
   - Security procedures:
     - Visitor processing. Are there guards present? Badges? What kind? Are access codes needed?
     - Unattended package/luggage. Leave a backpack to test reaction.
     - Unauthorized personnel or vehicles. People may drive to a checkpoint and claim they are lost.

Figure 2.4 Security responses.

- Security responses (Figure 2.4):
  - Alarm (fire, intrusion detection, etc.). The alarm could've been activated intentionally to test your and the emergency responders' reactions.
  - Bomb threat. This could be initiated to test your security reactions and to note the evacuation zones.

If you react to alarms, look for corollary activity that may indicate preattack surveillance. Is there someone videoing the event? Taking notes? It may be suspicious that someone just happened to be there to record the event. *Not normal.*

6. Measuring (Figure 2.5)
   - Measuring distance by pacing or "DUI walking."
   - Distance between vehicle bollards.
   - Distance between public transit drop-off area to entrance.
   - Distance from perimeter breach points to attack objective.
7. Timing (Figure 2.6)
   - Observe an event, look at watch, and take notes.

Figure 2.5 Measuring.

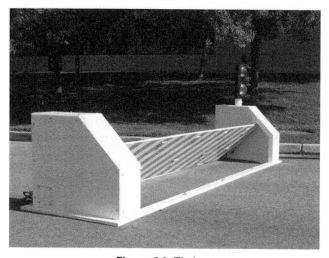

Figure 2.6 Timing.

- Shift change.
- Vehicle barriers. Raise and lower.
- VIP arrivals/departures.
- First responders' response times.
- Sensitive materials arrivals/departures.
8. Signaling
   - Nonverbal communication such as
     - Spray-painted symbols on walls or roads.
     - Flags or pennants.
     - Ribbons tied to sign posts.

— Signals that may indicate:
  ■ "The attack is a go."
  ■ "The VIP is in this car."
  ■ "This is where you blow yourself up."

One challenge for security officers is to distinguish between activities that are innocuous "normal" versus suspicious "not normal." People gathering at the bus stop outside your building may be part of a typical business day. *Normal.* One of them takes photos. Still *normal.* Later you notice the photographer is in the coffee shop across the street with a clear view of your building and is taking notes. He acts no different than any other customer at the shop. *Normal.* Then the photographer returns to take more photos of the comings and goings from the bus stop to your building's entrance. Taken individually, any one of these actions would be considered *normal*, but taken all together—*not normal.*

Other behaviors on their own may signify preattack surveillance. Someone spray painting an X on the sidewalk could be leaving a marker—*not normal.* Attempting covert photography in a "no photography zone" is definitely *not normal.* Someone pacing along your perimeter is *not normal.*

In all cases, trust your gut. Something may be suspicious that you can't yet recognize. Take the extra step to verify if it is "normal." Complacency is the enemy of vigilance. Always be on the lookout for the "not normal."

CASE STUDIES

CHAPTER OUTLINE

Abstract: Validated knowledge and experience are derived from observations and the historical study of training, exercises, and operations that lead to a change in behavior at the tactical (standing operating procedures, tactics, techniques, and procedures, etc.), operational, or strategic level domains. Information on these cases was extracted from several sources: (1) federal criminal court case records (indictments, Federal Bureau of Investigation affidavits, transcripts, etc.); (2) newspapers, books, and print media; and (3) other open source data to include Internet searches and other publicly available documents.

Keywords: activist, anarchist, Black Bloc, ecoterrorism, extremist, gang, radical, terrorist

You must learn from the mistakes of others. You can't possibly live long enough to make them all yourself.
Sam Levenson

Validated knowledge and experience are derived from observations and the historical study of training, exercises, and operations that lead to a change in behavior at the tactical [standing operating procedures, tactics, techniques, and procedures (TTPs), etc.], operational, or strategic level domains.

Information on these cases was extracted from several sources: (1) federal criminal court case records [indictments, Federal Bureau of Investigation (FBI) affidavits, transcripts, etc.]; (2) newspapers, books, and print media; and (3) other open source data to include Internet searches and other publicly available documents.

3.1 Criminals

Just about every criminal act from a mall parking lot mugging to robbing a bank is preceded by the criminal conducting some level of surveillance upon his target. Hollywood movies such as the casino heisting Ocean's 11 and "The Town" where a group of local men hit armored cars and the like carry Hollywood liberties, but nonetheless are good examples. They know the armored vehicle routes and the drivers and what type of weapons carried. They did their homework through surveillance to be successful—but more importantly to *not get caught!*

Different from terrorist surveillance, which has been show to last for weeks to months and even years, a criminal may surveil their targets for perhaps a few minutes or seconds before striking. Regardless, the criminal is in the open and can be detected prior to the attack. In South Africa, criminals have been known to target passengers and tour groups upon arrival at O.R. Tambo International Airport in Johannesburg. Typically, criminals receive word from inside operatives when "high-value" individuals are exiting the airport terminal. The victims are then followed and robbed at gunpoint upon arrival at their residence or hotel. An attacker's need for critical information about a target provides an opportunity for organizations to detect and disrupt an attack.

3.1.1 Anarchists

Many of us have at least heard of the *Anarchist Cookbook* first published in 1971 that contains instructions for the manufacture of explosives, rudimentary telecommunications devices, and other items. It was written by William Powell to protest the United States involvement in the Vietnam War, who has since denounced his original publication, saying "The book, in many respects, was a misguided product of my adolescent anger at the prospect of being drafted and sent to Vietnam to fight in a war that I did not believe in." Nevertheless, its current publisher and version is available to anyone for under $20.00 online. According to the FBI, between 1980 and 2001, approximately two-thirds of terrorism in the United States was carried out by non-Islamist extremists. From 2002 to 2005, this number jumped to 95%.

On May 1, 2012, the FBI arrested five individuals in a planned attack to blow up a Cleveland-area bridge and wage similar attacks upon a then-upcoming NATO summit. Surprisingly, this plot seemed to have no connection to Islamist extremism. Instead, three of the suspects were said to be self-proclaimed anarchists, and the motivation for the thwarted anarchists plot is largely where the difference ends.

The would-be attackers followed the pattern of the attack cycle by researching targets that were deemed attractive to their cause to destroy private property "to send a message to corporations." Moreover, an attack they could accomplish successfully without getting caught. The plotters conducted surveillance of many local critical infrastructures and settled on the Route 82 Brecksville–Northfield high-level bridge. This bridge crosses from Brecksville, Ohio to Sagamore Hills, Ohio over the Cuyahoga Valley National Park. Once they settled on their final target, the group went to the site on numerous occasions and took photos of the support structures of the bridge.

In several recent print and online communications and publications, radical anarchists of Spain boasted of their crimes against public and private property, as well as targeting certain individuals. They also openly discussed tactics and strategies for further disruptions, vandalism, and terror for imposing anarchist ideals on the public.

A Barcelona-based anarchist stated: "It's easy to attack…there are banks, real estate offices, car showrooms, airline offices, supermarkets, surveillance cameras, ticket machines in the metro, blank walls, advertisements." The anarchists encourage "more actions... carried out in broad daylight." The surrounding streets must first be watched by the perpetrators "to make sure there's no passing patrols," followed by "dedicating thirty seconds to your target... and disappearing into the multitude." Clandestine attacks at night are also necessary because "sometimes our goal is not to communicate but to cause damage, to sabotage...."

Several communications were collated in which Spanish anarchists listed attacks they saw as effective and successful. They were organized by tactics used and assets targeted, and over 400 cash machines throughout Barcelona were vandalized and put out of commission.

Police cars had their locks glued. Police stations have been stoned, as well.

Attacks involving paint bombs, fireworks, arson, hammers, or stones were perpetrated against employment agencies, a real estate office, and several banks, as well as a social security office and at least one municipality building. More than a dozen supermarkets had their locks glued in 1 day. Masked anarchists pulled various objects into the streets and set them on fire, shutting down major thoroughfares. In one case, over 200 people took part in road blockings in four different locations simultaneously in order to make law enforcement more difficult.

Several dozen anarchists blocked traffic and hung a banner from a bridge. Anarchists involved in the traffic blockage also slashed the tires of police vehicles. A tourist bus was targeted with paint bombs. An explosive was detonated outside a government building. A major passenger train line was blocked by a burning barricade on the tracks, while other rail sabotage included a steel cable tossed over the electric lines and incendiary devices detonated in the electrical and mechanical boxes along the tracks. On October 23, 2009, a group of 20 anarchists occupied the broadcast studios of Radio Cataluña in Barcelona, trying to read a communiqué on the air.

One sophisticated attack deserves separate mention: On October 5, 2009, anarchists in a neighborhood in Barcelona described as "perfect for an ambush" set dumpsters on fire and called the police. When two officers arrived at the scene and exited their car, they were pelted with rocks by attackers on a street higher up the hillside. The policemen were forced to retreat and the attackers smashed the patrol car's windows.

3.1.2 Violent Protesters

Over the centuries, organized societies often have spawned violent civil disturbances. Countless civil uprisings have been motivated by personal, religious, or political purposes, and many have prompted significant societal changes. Recent decades witnessed race riots across the United States in the 1960s, protests over American involvement in Vietnam in the 1970s, abortion clinic demonstrations in the 1980s, disturbances stemming from allegations of police brutality in the 1990s, and protests over American involvement in the Middle East in the 2000s. The Founding Fathers considered the right of the people to protest to be among the most fundamental rights accorded to humankind. The U.S. Constitution nearly failed ratification because the antifederalist coalition was concerned that no codification of the rights of the citizenry was included, prompting the Federalist coalition to develop the Bill of Rights.

Some serious criminal activities have been associated with public protest. The right to protest is acknowledged in law, but it is not unconditional. In particular, the public right to peaceful protest does not provide a defense for protesters who commit serious crime or disorder in pursuit of their objectives. Police face the challenge of identifying those individuals intent on causing crime and disruption, while simultaneously protecting the rights of those who wish to protest peacefully. Key to being able to differentiate between the two is reliable intelligence.

Intelligence helps those responsible for protecting communities from serious crime and disruption to make better decisions (and therefore to prevent crime) by improving their knowledge about the level and type of threat the public might face. The starting point for gathering such intelligence is prior reasonable suspicion that serious criminal acts may be in preparation.

It has been this author's personal experience from the impromptu protests that broke out across the United States (particularly San Francisco, CA) following the start of the second Gulf War that violent protesters are some of the most cunning and dedicated surveillants. A very detailed and illustrative booklet utilized commonly in the protester community provides exceptional understanding on how to conduct preprotest surveillance. Again, much of the information in this booklet focuses on ways not to get caught while conducting operational surveillance. Make no doubt about it, violent protesters have, will, and do conduct extensive surveillance of the locations and areas they intend to attack.

For informational purposes, the following presents some past known tactics, techniques, and procedures of "nonviolent" protest groups [Act Now to Stop War and End Racism (ANSWER), Greenpeace], affinity groups, and civil disobedient groups (Black Bloc).

Traditional activism that involves civil disobedience has developed a highly choreographed routine when it comes to getting arrested by the police. Lately, there have even been examples of where civil disobedience has generated into civil *obedience*, with activists negotiating with the police or even asking how to get arrested. ANSWER and other international and national protest organizations are highly organized and rely on smaller affinity groups (2—20 persons) to populate a planned protest. Many times during a large meeting, coordinated by ANSWER, of the smaller affinity groups (which can have 10—15 or more groups) a spokesperson or "spokes" represents the group and is asked which way the group would like to contribute [i.e., "Who wants to be arrested?" "Which group can contribute supplies for civil disobedience (paint, chains/handcuffs, wood for signs, etc.)?" Which group will videotape the protest for legal documentation of police brutality?" "Do we want to inundate the court system with arrests?" "Which group has attorneys working pro bono at the court house?"]. Most often, preprotest surveillance occurs the day or 2 days prior to the planned protest. Protesters are looking for unmovable objects to chain themselves to, escape routes if the protest is overwhelmed with police in riot gear, and exactly where to stage the protest for maximum effect.

Some of the TTPs for civil disobedience include the following.

- Using handcuffs/chains to form a human chain. To avoid bolt cutters, a large PVC pipe may be placed over the full length of each of the protester's arms. Protester A, with handcuff attached, places arm into pipe (approximately 5–6 in. diameter and 3–4 ft long) and protester B places hand and arm from other end and attaches handcuff inside the pipe. A circular saw, used commonly by emergency first responder personnel, has been used in the past to cut the pipe in two in order to get to the handcuff. Sometimes protesters will keep packets of fake blood in their hand, inside the pipe, to pretend being cut by the saw, complicating removal further. A group will surround an immovable object (building column, tree) and link themselves together.
- Die-ins are popular nonviolent civil unrest methods. Simple pretending to be dead, even when being arrested and placed into a vehicle.
- The throwing of paint is a common TTP. However, more serious groups have talked of using acids to damage property. It is unknown if decisions are made to use this TTP against law enforcement officer personnel.
- The ones to watch: Black Blocs are known for their use of innovative tactics that are unfamiliar to traditional activists (Figure 3.1). Black Bloc is not an organization, but a tactic of anarchistic persons. They typically stalk the

Figure 3.1 Black Bloc, Washington, DC.

outer perimeter of a protest looking for a prime opportunity to strike. Black Bloc persons do not want to be identified or arrested personally and will prolong or avoid illegal activity if the chance of arrest is apparent. Black Bloc individuals are usually identifiable easily by all-black clothing and disguising their faces with bandanas or cloth (Figure 3.2). The practice of "masking up" is controversial within activist circles. Some activists criticize mask wearing because it contradicts the image of activism being

Figure 3.2 Black Bloc, Sacramento, CA.

open and accessible—in other words, "We have nothing to hide." There are several reasons for wearing masks at an action: (1) to protect themselves from police surveillance; (2) to promote anonymity among the ranks, which helps protect against the rise of charismatic leaders; (3) to provide cover for activists engaged in illegal actions during the demonstration; and (4) to promote solidarity within the bloc. Common also are black patches with a large red letter "A" scrawled in the middle symbolizing the word anarchy. Backpacks are worn commonly and have been known to contain long lengths of heavy chain and heavy-duty locks, M-80 fireworks, Molotov cocktails, and fuse-initiated pipe bombs (Figure 3.3).

- Unarresting an activist(s) is quite simple—when an activist is arrested, the bloc of anarchists acts swiftly to pull that

Figure 3.3 Anarchist with Molotov cocktail.

person free from the police. Sometimes a tugging match is required to free the activist, but when they have the element of surprise, they can usually be successful because the police are so shocked that activists aren't playing the game correctly (i.e., negotiating their own imprisonment). Unarresting works in two situations: (1) when there are few police and several activists involved or (2) when the unarresting bloc outnumbers the officers by a ratio of 3:1 or better.

3.1.3 Gangs

Gangs, like all criminals, will not attack unless they feel they have the advantage. Their advantage is knowing all your movements and security protocols (and ways to defeat them) prior to the attack. The largest concern of gangs, outside of being in the wrong place at the wrong time during gang-on-gang violence or robbery, is kidnapping. Of course, this refers mainly to international gang activity, as kidnapping among U.S. gangs is not as prevalent. While this type of gang activity is known the world over, the major hub of gang kidnap activity occurs in Latin America countries. For instance, regarding El Salvador, many academics and political analysts conclude that the problem of gangs is the second most important sociological phenomenon of violence, after civil war. The high number of homicides—approximately 40 per 100,000 inhabitants—gives El Salvador the unenviable ranking as one of the most dangerous countries in Latin America.

Criminal street gang members, prison gang members, and individuals associated with transnational criminal organizations study books such as *The 48 Laws of Power* and Sun Tzu's *The Art of War* to understand military tactics and to prepare mentally for "war." Gang members may also enhance their knowledge and mental training by reading books such as *Blood in My Eye* (a book written by George Jackson, one of the founders of the prison gang Black Guerilla Family), *The Book of the Five Rings* (a book on kenjutsu and martial arts), and *The Turner Diaries* (a book written by William Pierce, former leader of the National Alliance—a white nationalist organization—and used by Timothy McVeigh in planning the bombing of the Alfred P. Murrah Federal Building in Oklahoma City).

MS-13 arrived in the United States having had ties to La Mara, a violent street gang in El Salvador. Many had actually seen fighting in El Salvador's civil war. Ex-members of the paramilitary Farabundo Marti para la LiberacionNacional (FMLN)[Farabundo Marti National Liberation Front] also numbered among the early founders of Mara Salvatrucha. Using guerilla tactics and urban terrorism, the FMLN had fought an insurgency against the Salvadoran government; as a result, many Salvadorans arrived in Los Angeles as "veterans," already adept in the use of explosives, firearms, and reconnaissance.

On January 31, 2009, in Pharr, Texas, an alleged gang member tossed a South Korean-made grenade into a bar with off-duty police officers. The grenade failed to explode due to the safety pin not being pulled properly. This is an example of targeted violence that certainly required a particular amount of surveillance and planning to know as much as possible about the target area and its intended victims. The grenade that failed to explode in the bar had the same markings as grenades thrown in October at the U.S. consulate in Monterrey, Mexico, and at a television station in early January in the same city. The grenade thrown at the consulate failed to explode, and no one was injured when the grenade hit the Televisa network's studio as it aired its nightly newscast. However, all three grenades were manufactured at the same time and place and were at one point together in the same batch from South Korea. After the grenade bounced off the floor and landed on a pool table, an off-duty police officer picked it up and threw it back out the door. No one was hurt, no arrests were made, and authorities are divided about whether the targets were rival gang members or off-duty police officers.

Gang recruitment of active-duty military personnel constitutes a significant criminal threat to the U.S. military. According to multiple law enforcement reportings, members of nearly every major street gang, as well as some prison gangs and outlaw motorcycle gangs, have been reported on both domestic and international military installations (Figure 3.4). Through transfers and deployments, military-affiliated gang members expand their culture and operations to new regions nationwide and worldwide, undermining security and law enforcement efforts to combat crime (Figure 3.5). Gang members with military training pose a unique threat to law enforcement personnel because of their distinctive weapons, combat training skills, and reconnaissance training and their ability to transfer these skills to fellow gang members.

Criminal gangs in Ireland and England are reportedly using reconnaissance units to stake

Figure 3.4 "Support your local Hells Angel" graffiti on a military vehicle in Iraq. Source: FBI.

Figure 3.5 A soldier in a combat zone throwing gang signs. Source: FBI.

out houses before leaving chalk markings outside denoting if they're ripe for burgling or too risky to enter. This method has also been known to be utilized by transient or "hobos" in the United States that travel illegally by train from place to place leaving signals for the next hobo to come through the area. It is understood at least eight signs are being used by the "recon unit," one of which indicates the occupant is a vulnerable female who is conned easily. Another points to the householder being nervous and afraid, while other signs indicate the house is a good target and its owners are wealthy. Reconnaissance units also save their burglar colleagues time by leaving signs showing there is nothing worth stealing from a house or that it is too risky to attempt burgling it (Figure 3.6).

3.1.4 Felons

Violent felons that fall into the routine of prison time have been known to be targeted by terrorist groups as they are introduced and radicalized in Islamic extremism. Years from now when criminologists write their textbooks on American terrorism, the name Kevin Lamar James may appear alongside such infamous figures as Timothy McVeigh, Ramzi Yousef, and Osama bin Laden. Kevin James was sentenced in February 2009 for conspiring to wage war against the United States. James pled guilty to the charge after he and three other men were indicted in 2005 for plotting to attack U.S. military facilities, Israeli government facilities, and Jewish synagogues in Los Angeles.

At the time of the indictments, the FBI described the plot as the most operationally advanced since September 11. Even more

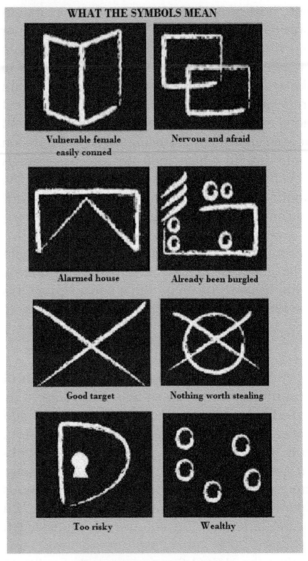

Figure 3.6 "Da *Pinchi* Code."

troubling is that James designed the plot while serving time in a California state prison. Prisoners, especially those in gangs, have long recruited other inmates to act as their collaborators upon release. James, however, was the first gang member to radicalize inmates into joining a prison gang with a terrorist agenda. A study funded by the National Institute of Justice (NIJ) and conducted by author Mark S. Hamm, Ph.D., took a closer look at the Kevin James case as part of a larger study on radicalization in prison. Three of the alleged conspirators—Levar Haney Washington, 26; Gregory Vernon Patterson, 22; and Hammad Riaz Samana, 22, a Pakistani national—confessed to 11 gas station robberies that the FBI alleges were perpetrated to finance terrorist attacks on military recruitment centers, synagogues, and the Israeli consulate. The fourth man indicted was Kevin Lamar James, 29, who had been housed in a California state prison in Sacramento since 1996 for committing a gang-related armed robbery. Terrorist shoe-bomber Richard Reid and Jose Padilla, who was held as an enemy combatant for attempting to detonate a "dirty bomb" before being charged with material support of terrorism and conspiracy to murder individuals in a foreign country, were both radicalized during stints in prison.

Levar Washington (Figure 3.7) grew up in South Los Angeles with dreams of becoming a rapper or a basketball star. Raised by his grandmother after being abandoned by his mother at age 13, he ended up in a gang and then in the custody of the California Youth Authority (CYA). Upon release from CYA, his criminal activity continued, as did his time in prison.

Washington converted to Islam while serving 3 years in Corcoran State Prison on a robbery conviction. While serving a subsequent sentence at High Desert State Prison, he was determined "violent and incorrigible" and was assigned to the highest level of security. Washington was at High Desert on September 11, 2001.

Figure 3.7 Levar Washington.

He reportedly met Jam'iyyat Ul-Islam Is-Saheeh, Arabic for "Assembly of Authentic Islam," founder and leader Kevin James while incarcerated at California State Prison in Sacramento. It is alleged that he took an oath of allegiance to James in November 2004, shortly before being paroled. James is alleged to have given Washington instructions to prepare for and then execute a terrorist attack on Los Angeles.

After his release, Washington worshipped at the Inglewood mosque. He reportedly held very radical views, which were not embraced by the leaders or members of the mosque.

It is believed that Washington met his two alleged accomplices, Gregory Patterson and Hamad Samana, at the Inglewood mosque. In late May 2005, Washington, Patterson, and Samana allegedly began surveilling and conducting a string of gas station robberies in and around Los Angeles. Initially, police made no connection between these robberies and any terrorist activities. On July 5, 2005, Washington and Patterson were arrested after Patterson dropped a cell phone at the scene of one of the crimes. A subsequent search of their apartment turned up bulletproof vests and jihadi materials not available readily via the Internet. Also found were the addresses of National Guard facilities, two synagogues, the Israeli consulate, and the El Al Airlines ticket counter at the Los Angeles airport.

Studies by the NIJ in 1999 revealed that terrorists are far more careful in planning and preparing for the completion of their attacks than other categories of criminal (as cited in Smith, Damphouse, & Roberts, 1999). This is due to the differing paradigms between both groups. While "average criminals" commit crimes with individualized self-serving motives, terrorists conduct attacks with religious, ideological, and/or political objectives in mind, which their parent organizations believe to serve the "greater good."

3.2 Terrorists

Over the past several decades, the United States has begun to articulate terrorism as a distinctive category of criminal activity. The United States Code (USC) uses several definitions of terrorism that address specific legal situations, all of which have entered into the legal lexicon only since the 1970s. The FBI subdivides the terrorist threat facing the United States into the broad categories of international and domestic terrorism, each of which involves violent acts intended to (1) intimidate or coerce a civilian population or (2) influence the policy or conduct of a government by mass destruction, assassination, or kidnapping. In cases of international terrorism, these acts transcend national boundaries in terms of the means by which they are accomplished, the persons they intend to intimidate, or the locale in which perpetrators operate [18 USC § 2331(1)]. In cases of domestic terrorism, the FBI defines the source of coercion as a group or individual based and operating entirely within the United States, or its territories, without foreign direction [18 USC § 2331(5)]. These legal definitions revolve around terrorism as coercion—as a violent means to a political end.

There is no single, universally accepted, definition of terrorism. Terrorism is defined in the U.S. Code of Federal Regulations as "the unlawful use of force and violence against persons or property to intimidate or coerce a government, the civilian population, or any segment thereof, in furtherance of political or social objectives" (28 C.F.R. Section 0.85).

For the purpose of this book, let's use the FBI's definitions of domestic terrorism and international terrorism:

- *Domestic terrorism* is the unlawful use, or threatened use, of force or violence by a group or individual based and operating entirely within the United States or Puerto Rico without foreign direction committed against persons or property to intimidate or coerce a government, the civilian population, or any segment thereof in furtherance of political or social objectives.
- *International terrorism* involves violent acts or acts dangerous to human life that are a violation of the criminal laws of the United

States or any state, or that would be a criminal violation if committed within the jurisdiction of the United States or any state. These acts appear to be intended to intimidate or coerce a civilian population, influence the policy of a government by intimidation or coercion, or affect the conduct of a government by assassination or kidnapping. International terrorist acts occur outside the United States or transcend national boundaries in terms of the means by which they are accomplished, the persons they appear intended to coerce or intimidate, or the locale in which their perpetrators operate or seek asylum.

3.2.1 International

3.2.1.1 Professional/State Sponsored

Khobar Towers

At 2149 hours on June 25, 1996, security police sentries posted on the roof top of Building 131 observed a septic tank truck and car traveling east bound in the parking lot just outside the north perimeter fence. When the truck was abeam Building 131, it turned left away from the compound. The truck then began to back up into the hedges just outside the fence. Occupants of the truck jumped in the waiting car and sped off. Sentries radioed the situation into the security desk and began alerting building occupants in Building 131 of Khobar Towers.

One American sentry, Air Force Staff Sergeant Alfredo R. Guerrero, stationed atop Building 131, witnessed the men, recognized the vehicles as a threat, and began a floor-by-floor evacuation of the building. His actions are credited with saving dozens of lives. Many of the evacuees were in the stairwell when the bomb went off. The stairwell was constructed of heavy marble and was located on the side of the building away from the truck bomb, perhaps the safest location in the building. For his actions, Guerrero was awarded the Airman's Medal, the U.S. Air Force's highest peacetime award for valor. While working for the Department of Defense, the author of this book had the distinct honor of having Al Guerrero as one of his antiterrorism level II instructors.

At 2155 hours, the bomb detonated. Estimates of the bomb's size vary. One estimate states the bomb was equivalent to 3000–8000 pounds of TNT, but was most likely 5000 pounds. Another estimate puts the bomb size at 20,000–30,000 pounds of TNT.

Nineteen American service personnel were killed and more than 200 injured. Hundreds of Saudi citizens and third-country nationals (TCN) living in the complex and immediate vicinity were also injured; some were probably killed. The bomb blast blew out windows throughout the compound and created a crater 85 feet wide and 35 feet deep. The blast was felt in Bahrain, 20 miles away. This was a watershed event for Department of Defense Antiterrorism Force Protection.

From the UNITED STATES DISTRICT COURT EASTERN DISTRICT OF VIRGINIA ALEXANDRIA DIVISION indictment:

In about 1993, AL-MUGHASSIL instructed
AL-QASSAB, AL-YACOUB, and AL-HOURI to begin
surveillance of Americans in Saudi Arabia. As a result,

AL-QASSAB and AL-YACOUB spent three months in Riyadh conducting surveillance of American targets. AL-SAYEGH joined them during this operation. They produced reports, which were passed to AL-MUGHASSIL, then on to Saudi Hizballah chief AL-NASSER, and to officials in Iran. At the end of their mission, AL-MUGHASSIL came in person to meet with them and review their work.

Also in about 1993, AL-YACOUB assigned AL-JARASH to conduct surveillance of the United States Embassy in Riyadh, Saudi Arabia, and to determine where Americans went and where they lived. Also at AL-YACOUB's direction, AL-JARASH and ALMARHOUN conducted surveillance of a fish market frequented by Americans, located near the U.S. Embassy in Riyadh. They reported the results of their surveillance to AL-YACOUB.

In early 1994, AL-QASSAB began conducting surveillance, focusing on American and other foreign sites in the eastern province of Saudi Arabia, an area that includes Khobar. He prepared written reports, which were passed to AL-NASSER and Iranian officials.

In about Fall 1994, AL-MARHOUN, RAMADAN, and AL-MU'ALEM began watching American sites in Eastern Saudi Arabia at AL-MUGHASSIL's direction. They passed their reports to AL-MUGHASSIL, who was then spending most of his time in Beirut, Lebanon. At about the same time, AL-BAHAR began conducting surveillance in Saudi Arabia at the direction of an Iranian military officer.

In late 1994, after extensive surveillance in Eastern Saudi Arabia, ALMARHOUN, RAMADAN, and AL-MU'ALEM recognized and confirmed Khobar Towers as an important American military location and communicated that fact to AL-MUGHASSIL. Shortly thereafter, AL-MUGHASSIL gave RAMADAN money to find a storage site in the eastern province for explosives. During the course of the cell's surveillance, AL-MUGHASSIL reported to AL-MARHOUN that he had received a phone call from a high Iranian government official inquiring about the progress of their surveillance activity.

Iranian military officer of the area of Jizan, Saudi Arabia, located on the Red Sea near Yemen; they also surveilled American sites in the eastern province. Their goal was to gather information to support future attacks against Americans. AL-SAYEGH took their surveillance reports and passed them to the Iranian officer.

In about April or May 1995, AL-MARHOUN attended four days of live-fire drills sponsored by Hizballah in Lebanon. While he was there, he met with AL-MUGHASSIL at his Beirut apartment. During that meeting, AL-MUGHASSIL explained to AL-MARHOUN that Hizballah's goal was to expel the Americans from Saudi Arabia. AL-MUGHASSIL also explained that he had close ties to Iranian officials, who supplied him with money and gave him directions for the party. AL-MUGHASSIL then gave AL-MARHOUN $2000 in $100 United States bills to support AL-MARHOUN's cell in their surveillance activity in Saudi Arabia. ALMARHOUN used the money to finance a trip to Riyadh with RAMADAN to look for American sites.

In about June 1995, the Hizballah cell composed of AL-MARHOUN, RAMADAN, and AL-MU'ALEM began regular surveillance of Khobar Towers at ALMUGHASSIL's direction. Shortly thereafter, RAMADAN traveled to Beirut to brief ALMUGHASSIL, who instructed the cell to continue surveillance. At about the same time in 1995 that RAMADAN went to Beirut to update ALMUGHASSIL on surveillance activities, AL-ALAWE was summoned to Beirut by ALMUGHASSIL. Although AL-ALAWE did not see RAMADAN, he noticed surveillance reports from RAMADAN on AL-MUGHASSIL's desk. During their meeting, AL-MUGHASSIL explained to AL-ALAWE that explosives were going to be used against Americans in Saudi Arabia and he instructed AL-ALAWE to drive a vehicle he said contained explosives from Lebanon to Saudi Arabia. AL-ALAWE did so, only to discover that the car held no explosives; AL-MUGHASSIL explained that he had only been testing him.

In about October 1995, an unknown man visited AL-ALAWE at his home in eastern Saudi Arabia and

*delivered a map of Khobar, saying AL-MUGHASSIL
wanted ALALAWE to check its accuracy. A short time
later, the same man retrieved the map and left
a package weighing about one kilogram.*

In Summary:

*In about 1993, AL-QASSAB, AL-YACOUB, and
AL-SAYEGH conducted surveillance of American
targets in Riyadh, Saudi Arabia.*

*In about 1993, AL-YACOUB assigned AL-JARASH to
conduct surveillance of the United States Embassy in
Riyadh, Saudi Arabia, and instructed him to determine
where Americans went and where they lived.*

*In about 1993, at AL-YACOUB's direction, AL-JARASH
and AL-MARHOUN conducted surveillance of a fish
market frequented by Americans, located near the
U.S. embassy in Riyadh.*

*In early 1994, AL-QASSAB began conducting
surveillance focusing on American and other foreign
sites in the eastern province of Saudi Arabia.*

*In about the fall of 1994, AL-MARHOUN, RAMADAN,
and AL-MU'ALEM, working as a group, began
watching American sites in Eastern Saudi Arabia at
ALMUGHASSIL's direction.*

*In about the fall of 1994, AL-BAHAR began
conducting surveillance in Saudi Arabia at the
direction of an Iranian military officer.*

*In late 1994, following extensive surveillance in
Eastern Saudi Arabia, ALMARHOUN, RAMADAN,
and AL-MU'ALEM recognized and confirmed Khobar
Towers as an important American military location
and communicated that fact to AL-MUGHASSIL.*

*In late 1994 or early 1995, AL-MUGHASSIL gave
RAMADAN money to find a storage site in the eastern
province for explosives.*

*In 1995, AL-BAHAR and HANI AL-SAYEGH conducted
surveillance at the direction of an Iranian military
officer of the area of Jizan, Saudi Arabia.*

*In 1995, AL-BAHAR and HANI AL-SAYEGH conducted
surveillance of American sites in the eastern province.*

In about April or May 1995, AL-MARHOUN met in Beirut with ALMUGHASSIL, who gave AL-MARHOUN $2000 in $100 United States bills to support ALMARHOUN's cell in their surveillance activity in Saudi Arabia.

In about June 1995, the Hizballah cell, composed of AL-MARHOUN, RAMADAN, and AL-MU'ALEM, began intense surveillance of Khobar Towers at ALMUGHASSIL's direction.

In about mid-1995, RAMADAN traveled to Beirut to brief AL-MUGHASSIL, who instructed the cell to continue surveillance.

From April through June 1996, the security police reported 10 incidents of possible surveillance of the Khobar Towers (Figure 3.8).

These incidents were investigated by the Air Force Office of Special Investigations, the Saudi

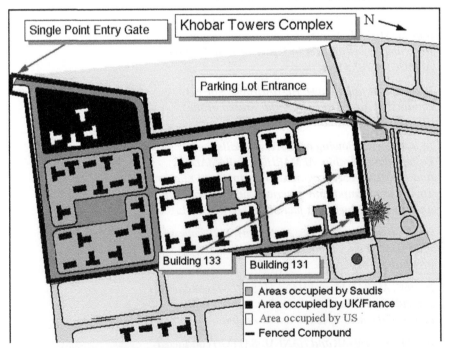

Figure 3.8 Map overlay of the military compound in Dhahran, Saudi Arabia.

military police, and local civilian police. Five incidents were explained and dismissed. Four incidents were reports of surveillance where the vehicle used in the getaway was sighted as Middle Eastern men who drove by or parked and observed the compound. Saudi police thought this was not uncommon due to curiosity and an increased number of people in the area during the Hajj season.

One incident in May was a possible threat indicator when a Jersey barrier on the east perimeter was rammed by a slow-moving car. The driver very likely may have been testing to see if the barrier could be moved. This test of the barrier reinforced to the wing leaders that a penetration attack was the most likely threat. Force protection actions taken included staking all Jersey barriers down with steel rods, stringing more concertina wire on perimeters, compiling a list to monitor TCN workers, obtaining night vision scopes for observation posts, briefing residents of Buildings 131 and 133 to maintain increased vigilance, training explosive detection dogs by explosive ordnance disposal personnel using 250-pound category bombs, increasing security police posts to 13 for day and 15 for night, initiating roof-top observation posts at night, updating building evacuation plans, and coordinating with the Saudis to implement a procedure to check license plates of suspicious vehicles.

After action reports and investigations detail the intense preoperational surveillance efforts of the attackers:

• Saudi Hezbollah three-person surveillance team

- Conducted preattack surveillance operations against various U.S. targets in the city of Dhahran
- Conducted 40 dedicated preattack surveillance missions against Khobar
- Began on-ground operations 21 months prior to the attack
- Several of the sightings of suspected surveillance came from two minarets that had direct line of sight of the buildings and compound (Figure 3.9).

Dhiren Barot

British-born Muslim convert Dhiren Barot (Figure 3.10), aka Abu Issa al-Hindi, surveilled economic targets in the New York City financial district, as well as Newark, New Jersey, and Washington, DC, in April 2001 after he was

Figure 3.9 Minarets used for surveillance. The crater remaining after the truck bomb explosion is evident with Building 131 on the right.

Figure 3.10 Dhiren Barot.

directed to do so by 9/11 attack mastermind Khalid Sheikh Mohammed (aka KSM). This was done as part of a possible second round of attacks that KSM envisioned for some time in the future after 9/11. Barot, using a student visa, reportedly applied to a New York area college in June 2000; even though he was admitted to that school in 2000–2001, he never enrolled or attended any classes at that college. Barot reportedly lived in New Jersey, using his student status as a cover.

This cover apparently worked well, as the surveillance plans he outlined reportedly were very detailed. They included descriptions of what vehicles would be able to enter the basement of the Prudential building, potential getaway routes (implying they were not suicide attacks), and notes on a visit to Newark City Hall to (unsuccessfully) gather blueprints. Barot was not arrested in the United States, however, but in the United Kingdom in early August 2004, soon after the July arrest of alleged al Qaeda operative and computer expert Mohammed Naeem Noor Khan in Pakistan, who reportedly had copies of the surveillance plans on his computer and compact disks. The discovery led U.S. Department of Homeland Security (DHS) officials to declare an "orange alert" for the financial sector on August 1, 2004, even though the casing reports were old.

He flew to the New York area twice from the United Kingdom: first from August 17 to November 14, 2000, with conspirator Nadeem Tarmohamed; and again from March 11 to April 8, 2001, with Tarmohamed and Qaisar Shaffi. According to a Department of Justice indictment, during this time they visited and conducted surveillance:

> . . . on buildings and surrounding neighborhoods in the United States, including the International Monetary Fund World Headquarters and the World Bank Headquarters in Washington, D.C., the Prudential Corporate Plaza and World Headquarters Building in Newark, New Jersey, and the New York Stock Exchange Building and the Citigroup Center in Manhattan, New York. This surveillance allegedly included, among other things, video surveillance conducted in Manhattan in or about April 2001. The indictment alleges that the surveillance was part of the conspiracy to use weapons of mass destruction.

In addition to surveillance tapes, Barot kept specific notes about security in and around the targeted buildings (Figure 3.11):

- At Citicorp, for example, he mapped the best place to plant bombs, kept track of security

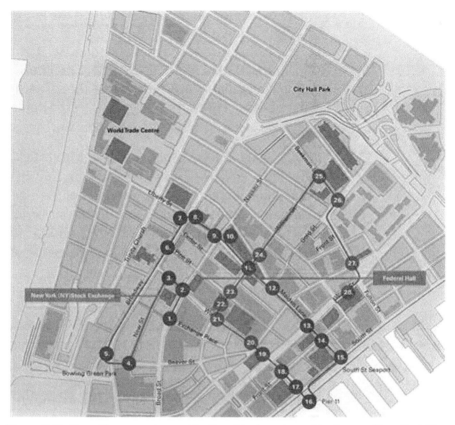

Figure 3.11 Surveillance route used by Barot in downtown Manhattan, New York City, April 2001. Source: London Met Police.

personnel and times of heaviest pedestrian flow, and highlighted exact times and locations of when puppet shows for children are held in the building's atrium.

• At the stock exchange, he had detailed information on the building itself. He timed traffic lights and patterns and mapped out detailed escape routes for bombers through subway and sewage tunnels.

• At the Prudential building, he had the exact location of the garage, timed traffic lights around the building, and suggested driving and exploding an oil tanker through the lobby to bring down the building.

- As previously released documents show, Barot planned to use gas-filled limousines as bombs. The document also refers to the Madrid bombings of March 11, 2004 as a "respectable project" that "deserved to be emulated."

In a 2006 story highlighted by a Metro U.K. newspaper, terror plotter Dhiren Barot and his alleged coconspirators had clearly been trained in antisurveillance techniques. On one occasion, the two of them traveled from London to Swansea just to use an Internet cafe before driving straight back.

Prosecutor Edmund Lawson QC told Woolwich Crown Court: "They were plainly surveillance conscious and they plainly received training or instruction from someone on the use of anti-surveillance techniques" (Figures 3.12 and 3.13). Even though they all had mobile telephones, there was only one occasion when they were seen to speak by phone over a period of months, the court heard. "When they met, it seems that the meeting sites were often deliberately chosen to make observation difficult, if not impossible," Mr. Lawson said. "They would meet in parks or reservoirs and walk around in the open air to have their discussions."

Barot and others set up Yahoo e-mail accounts to send coded messages to each other, the prosecutor said. "They used code in their communications… a code which has not yet been cracked such as to yield material such as could be used evidentially," Mr. Lawson said. "These were written in the style of teenagers discussing music, television, etc etera, and using incoming vehicles and the other for outgoing ones. Between these two entrances there is a single bar barrier partition that separates them.

- The car park is usually manned by ▮ members of security ▮▮▮▮▮▮▮. ▮▮▮▮▮▮▮▮ They are equipped with wireless radio communication sets.
- It is an open car park, i.e. there are no shutters that need to be lifted for entry/exit. It is mostly frequented by limousines.
- The height of the car park entrance/exit states 6''0 (I am assuming that this means 6 foot, but it appears to be more like 7 feet) – as is written above the entrance. It is probably adequate for a transit van to fit through but unsuitable for a courier vehicle.
- After the car park there is a loading bay (it is not very deep).

- The glass on the building appears to be double glazed, if not heavy duty since it is quite thick.

- **Main Entrance:** Inside the main entrance lobby area, directly on the right hand side is a large reception desk that more resembles a security counter. There are ▮▮▮▮ personnel on duty there. All of them are wearing security uniforms and are anything but receptionists. Most are male.
- Even further right, past the security desk, there is a posh seating area.
- There are several metal turnstile barriers that must be passed if a person wishes to venture into the main building beyond the lobby. Behind these turnstiles there is a large number of security personnel. More so than other similar institutions.
- Past the turnstiles, on the right hand side there is an eastern life size idol statue.
- After the barriers there are marble stairs that lead upwards (See, previous photo) above which there is a crystal chandelier hanging from the ceiling.
- It is a very elegant place with marble floors.

- **Atrium:** There is an atrium located directly in the center of the building. It is 100 x 140 ft (entire space). (See, 'IMF' folder for *Plan* photo. Also see, 'Interiors' folder for all *Atrium* photos).

Since the general public is not allowed into the building, it (the Atrium) appears to be private, for use by personnel only. For your information, a fire broke out in the atrium in the 1970s, for further reading on this refer to the *Plan* photo, and also the *Published Comments section* near end of this presentation for specific reading.
- **Rooms:** Many of the top officials' rooms are inward facing since this building is slightly unconventional in that it breaks with tradition by have an interior court/atrium. ▮▮▮▮▮▮▮▮▮▮▮▮▮▮▮▮▮▮▮▮▮▮

- It is a very large-scale area, and the ceiling is even higher than that of the *IMF Center* (see below for further details regarding this place).

- There are no garbage bins near the building.

15

Figure 3.12 Barot targeting package of World Bank IMF; page 15 of a 35-page report. Note the amount of detail in the report.

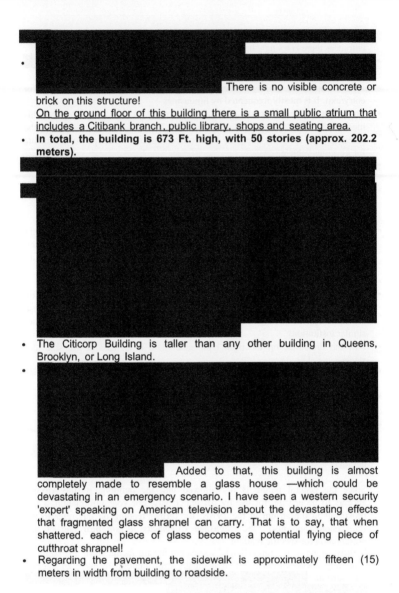

- There is no visible concrete or brick on this structure!
On the ground floor of this building there is a small public atrium that includes a Citibank branch, public library, shops and seating area.
- **In total, the building is 673 Ft. high, with 50 stories (approx. 202.2 meters).**

- The Citicorp Building is taller than any other building in Queens, Brooklyn, or Long Island.

- Added to that, this building is almost completely made to resemble a glass house —which could be devastating in an emergency scenario. I have seen a western security 'expert' speaking on American television about the devastating effects that fragmented glass shrapnel can carry. That is to say, that when shattered. each piece of glass becomes a potential flying piece of cutthroat shrapnel!
- Regarding the pavement, the sidewalk is approximately fifteen (15) meters in width from building to roadside.

12

Figure 3.13 Barot targeting package of Citigroup NYC; page 12 of a 17-page report. Note mention of devastating effects of glass as shrapnel.

language and employing sexual references which would not normally be considered appropriate to devout Muslims."

The three e-mail addresses highlighted to the court were kewl-n-kinki@yahoo.co.uk, which Mr. Lawson said was used by Barot, and two others used by codefendants bridget-jonesdiaries@yahoo.co.uk and nightwithkylie@yahoo.co.uk. About 30 messages were sent between these addresses during the period they were under surveillance, the court heard. Mr. Lawson said one seemed to contain a coded warning to the recipient to avoid being followed by police.

Sent from the nightwithkylie address to the bridget-jones address the day before Barot was arrested, it read: "make sure u don't bring your friend the 1 who loves listening 2 red hot chillie. u know I don't like her at all." Mr Lawson said: "It appears to be a warning on its own to make sure that you are not tailed." Another message between the same addresses read like a love note, he continued. It began: "baby tears, nice 1 love, u know that I can never let you down, especially you." The QC told the court: "Whatever else that was, it was not a love letter." He went on: "One extreme example of the use of email by Barot was that (two codefendants) traveled hundreds of miles to Swansea solely for the purpose of using an Internet cafe, then returned to London." The 400-mile round trip was "entirely idiotic" and could "only have been to seek to avoid surveillance," he added.

In a surprise move on October 12, 2006, Barot pled guilty to conspiracy in the plot to blow up the New York Stock Exchange and the other high-profile U.S. financial targets he had reportedly surveilled, along with plotting to conduct attacks in the United Kingdom.

Mumbai

On November 26, 2008, terrorist masterminds executed an intricate attack on India's financial and entertainment capital, Mumbai (Figure 3.14). With a series of synchronized and strategically placed bombs, India's largest city was set ablaze, killing 173 people and wounding 308 more. At approximately 2000 hours, two motorized inflatable boats containing five men, each belonging to the terrorist group Lashkar-e-Taiba (LeT), landed on the southern tip of the peninsula jutting into the Arabian Sea—home to nearly 21 million citizens of Mumbai city, formerly known as Bombay. Armed only with small arms (AK-47s) and hand grenades, they proceeded up the peninsula

Figure 3.14 Aftermath of the Mumbai Attack.

conducting terrorist attacks. By 0800 hours on November 29, Indian Rapid Action Force personnel, Marine commandos, and National Security Guard forces had killed nine of the attackers and captured Pakistani citizen Ajmal Kasab.

Elevator closed-circuit television (CCTV) footage captured the terrorists attempting to operate an elevator during the early stages of the 3-day siege (Figure 3.15). They were attempting to take the elevator down by jumping up over the door to hit the "down" arrow. They didn't know how to operate an elevator because they had never been in an elevator before. They finally discovered the buttons to go down and, to their apparent adulation, were able get the elevator to work to then attack the security command center in the lower levels of the Taj Hotel.

The attackers received reconnaissance assistance before the attacks. Ajmal Kasab, the only attacker who was captured alive, later confessed

Figure 3.15 Taj Hotel CCTV showing the attackers entering the elevator bank.

Figure 3.16 Lone surviving LeT-trained gunman Ajmal Amir Kasab.

upon interrogation that the attacks were conducted with the support of Pakistan's ISI (Figures 3.16 and 3.17). Kasab reported that for the approximate equivalent to $1500.00 USD to his family he became a trained terrorist intent on martyrdom. Kasab's disclosures subsequently helped with the arrest of several other Lashkar

Figure 3.17 CCTV of Mumbai Attacker.

operatives, such as David Headley, the American who was sentenced to serve 35 years' imprisonment in Chicago. It was very unfortunate for LeT that Kasab was apprehended and then revealed details of the group.

Headley's role in the terror attack included the following (Figure 3.18):

- Starting in 2002 and continuing into 2005, Headley attended five separate Lashkar training camps where he was indoctrinated on the merits of waging jihad and trained in combat skills.
- At the instance of LeT leaders, he changed his given name of Dawood Gilani and enlisted the assistance of his friend Tahawwur Hussain Rana to travel to and stay in Mumbai without detection starting in 2006 and continuing into 2008.

Figure 3.18 This photo was taken July 1, 2008, upon Headley's arrival at Mumbai's airport for his last reconnaissance trip. On November 26, he watched on television from Lahore as attackers used his information to navigate their brutal siege of Mumbai. Source: PBS Frontline.

- Headley provided video of and intelligence about the locations that later were targeted during the Mumbai attacks.
- Headley also assisted in plotting out a portion of the nautical route that the attackers would take and recommended the landing point that they later used to enter Mumbai without being detected.
- After seeing what took place in Mumbai in November 2008, Headley traveled to Denmark in January 2009. There, he gained entry to two separate facilities for the newspaper, using the same cover story provided to him that he used in Mumbai.
- Before each trip, Lashkar members and associates instructed Headley regarding specific locations where he was to conduct surveillance.
- After each trip, Headley traveled to Pakistan to meet with Lashkar members and associates, report on the results of his surveillance, and provide surveillance videos.
- Before the April 2008 surveillance trip, Headley and co-conspirators in Pakistan discussed potential landing sites in Mumbai for a team of attackers who would arrive by sea.
- Headley returned to Mumbai with a global positioning system (GPS) device and took boat trips around the Mumbai harbor, entering various locations into the device.
- Headley trips included the TajMahal and Oberoi hotels, the Leopold Cafe, the Chabad House, and the Chhatrapati Shivaji Terminus train station, each of which Headley had scouted in advance.
- In March 2009, Headley made a sixth trip to India to conduct additional surveillance, including the National Defence College in Delhi and Chabad Houses in several cities.

According to his plea agreement, Headley made trips to Mumbai to conduct surveillance in September 2006, February and September 2007, and April and June 2008. On each occasion, posing as a tourist, he took extensive videos that he delivered to his LeT and ISI handlers in Pakistan. He did not learn of the planned assault from the sea until just before his April 2008 trip to Mumbai, when potential landing sites were discussed. After arriving in Mumbai in April 2008, Headley identified the various landing sites with GPS, traveling by boat to each one so he could further describe the sites upon his return to Pakistan.

Video became essential to the surveillance phase of the operation. In fact, when doing his surveillance activities throughout the city, Headley stayed frequently at the Taj Mahal Palace Hotel, eventually a prime target, going on in-house tours and photographing and shooting surveillance videos. By the time he finished his surveillance there, he had documented almost every square inch of the very large hotel. In addition to the Taj Mahal Palace Hotel, the final targets were the Leopold Café, the Chabad House Jewish Community Center, the Chhatrapati Shivaji Terminus train station, and the Oberoi-Trident Hotel. The Oberoi was considered a target of opportunity because it had not been on Headley's original list of potential targets; however, he took an opportunity to video the hotel and it was eventually selected for the attack.

Why these targets were eventually selected is subject to speculation. However, the fact that Mumbai has nearly 22 million people in one of the world's most populated countries guarantees immediate publicity, which is what terrorist groups thrive on. Without media coverage, the event would never get noticed, nor would the terrorist group's political message be conveyed to the general public. The two hotels attacked are some of the largest in the city and traditionally host many foreigners. It can be assumed that these hotels were chosen for maximum casualties. The Jewish community center appears to have been a target because of the traditional animosity between Muslims and Jews. The Leopold Café is a popular restaurant and bar hangout for foreigners. Drinking and bars are against Muslim religious practices, so it is possible that the bar was chosen as a target because of its affront to Islam. Finally, the train station was an excellent target because of the large number of Indian passengers frequently present in its terminal.

Over 21 months of extremely detailed surveillance occurred in preparation for the attack. The terrorist knew the target locations and city better than the local police—the most incredible point to this is that *the attack team had never step foot in the city*. How is it that these nine individuals could conduct such a successful attack and hold a major city siege for 3 days at 10 different locations, never stepping a foot in the city? It was all done with extensive surveillance of videotaping, watching, querying, measuring, probing, and planning for the attack—all accomplished over an extended period of time under the nose of security forces not trained to look for unusual and suspicious activities of a terrorist surveillance team. Had those security forces understood what to look for and had a reporting system in place to collate the suspicious activity, the possibility of realizing an attack was in development could have allowed them to deter and even prevent this massacre from taking place.

3.2.1.2 Amateurs, Wannabes, and Lone Wolves
Anders Behring Breivik, Oslo, Norway

Anders Behring Breivik, a Norwegian, killed 77 people in a bombing and shooting rampage in Oslo and on Utoya Island, a summer camp for young political activists, on July 22, 2011 (Figure 3.19).

Breivik, a right-wing extremist, admitted to the slayings in a court hearing shortly afterward, but denied criminal guilt, portraying the victims as "traitors" for embracing multiculturalism and Muslim immigration policies. On August 24, 2012, a Norwegian court sentenced Breivik to 21

Figure 3.19 Anders Behring Breivik.

years in prison after ruling that he had been sane at the time of the massacre. The sentence is the longest provided by Norwegian law.

Breivik's presurveillance activities are noteworthy; however, what is of particular interest was his meticulous and extreme measures to ensure he did not get caught in his preattack planning and logistics phase, most of which can be found in his manifesto entitled *2083: A European Declaration of Independence*, which is 1518 pages long, bearing the name "Andrew Berwick." The file was e-mailed to 1003 addresses about 90 minutes before the bomb blast in Oslo—a terrorists ideal template for future attackers wrought with specifics—therein ensuring that like-minded (and nonlikeminded) groups and individuals are able to study and learn from his successful attack. He also encouraged his more than 7000 Facebook friends to use his manifesto as a blueprint for action. In many places, Breivik's writings are less a true manifesto than a straight-up diary in which he documents the months of planning that preceded his attacks:

> Our challenge is to get through and to know where and how to hide, leaving the enemy bewildered in areas he doesn't know. Being familiar with the avenues, streets, alleys, ins and outs, the corners of the urban centers, its paths and shortcuts, its empty lots, its underground passages, its pipes and sewer systems, the urban resistance fighter safely crosses through the irregular and difficult terrain unfamiliar to the police, where the police can be surprised in a fatal ambush or trap at any moment.

> Because he knows the terrain, the Justiciar Knight can pass through it on foot, on bicycle, in a car, and never be trapped. The Justiciar Knight must know the way in detail, and, in this manner, must go through the

schedule ahead of time as a training, to avoid entering alleyways that have no exit.[1]

The revolutionary method of carrying out actions is strongly and forcefully based on the knowledge and use of the following elements;

1. Financing your operation
2. Safe research and intelligence gathering
3. Acquirement of weapons, body armour and other equipment
4. Transportation (having a car/scooter available or rely on expropriation)
5. Safe storage in remote caches (the elimination of evidence)
6. Reconnaissance or exploration of the terrain
7. Study and timing of routes
8. Simulate the operation again and again (study and practice)
9. Success

The car bomb Breivik detonated at the Government Quarter weighed about 2100 pounds (950 kilograms), and its main components were fertilizer and diesel. Breivik used online recipes to build it and purchased the ingredients from retailers in Norway and abroad. He ordered 6 tons of fertilizer from the Norwegian cooperative Felleskjøpet on May 4, 2011. The aluminum powder—a core ingredient in fertilizer bombs—was bought online from a Polish company. Breivik originally wanted to build three bombs, but realized he was running short of time and finances so decided to make only one. After July 22, police found great quantities of leftover bomb-making materials at Breivik's farm.

---

[1] *2083: A European Declaration of Independence, Anders Behring Breivik.*

Most of Breivik's special equipment was purchased on eBay, including a tactical rifle fore grip from a Hong Kong-based trader, a zoom spotting scope from a Chinese supplier, and a LaserLyte pistol bayonet from a U.S.-based retailer. He also bought 15 vinyl air bags that may have been used to stabilize the car bomb during transport.

As for the weapons Breivik used on July 22, his initial plan was to buy them on the black market in countries he considered "European criminal network hubs." This somewhat naive idea led Breivik into one of his tactical misfortunes as he drove all the way to the Czech Republic to actively approach people he believed to be criminals. In his book, which is also known as his "compendium," he described the trip as a complete failure as everyone he approached thought he was crazy. He therefore lost his motivation and returned empty-handed. Surprisingly, acquiring weapons legally in Norway proved much easier than buying them on the black market abroad. Breivik simply used his hunting license and pistol club membership to buy a Ruger Mini 14 (semiautomatic rifle) and a 9-mm Glock 17 (semiautomatic pistol).

Incidents suggest that Breivik may not have been as cool-headed as is commonly portrayed. For instance, he was kicked out of a bar in Oslo a year before the attacks, having annoyed a Norwegian celebrity by talking extensively about crusades, Islam, and Templar Knights. While being escorted out of the bar, he reportedly shouted at the celebrity: "A year from now, I will be three times as famous as you!" Moreover, in March 2011, Breivik apparently called the central switchboard of Norwegian ministries, threatening to kill members of The Workers' Youth League at Utøya. This incident was logged, but never forwarded to the Police Secret Service as it was considered an empty threat. Breivik later acknowledged making the call, but said he does not remember its contents.

Finally, not everything went according to Breivik's plan on the day of the attacks. His original idea was to be in Oslo and start the distribution of the compendium at 3:00 AM the night before and to detonate the vehicle around 10:00 AM. The bomb, however, was not detonated until 3:25 PM. The precise reasons for the delay are not clear. Breivik himself claims to have been delayed back at the farm and not having made it to Oslo until 11:00 PM, after which he went to sleep because he was tired. It has later become known, however, that Breivik, on the night before the attacks, visited the same bar in Oslo from which he had been kicked out of a year before.

In any case, Breivik did not wake until 8:00 AM the next morning; he started the day by installing a new computer modem and configuring Microsoft Outlook on his personal computer, presumably in preparation for the e-mail distribution. This took more time than expected, which caused him to panic slightly. He decided to go on an additional reconnaissance trip to the Government Quarter before returning to his mother's home to upload the movie trailer on YouTube. He claims that he wrote the last message in the compendium at 2:45 PM. When he finally decided to initiate his plan, many people had already left work at the Government

Quarter. In his own mind, he failed his first mission because he was delayed and not enough people were killed. During an interview, he claims that he could have surrendered immediately if more people would have been killed in the first attack.

In July 2010, Breivik wrote he had "successfully finished the 'armour acquisition phase,'" including buying a protective case to store the weapons underground in a forest that was a 2-hour drive away from his farm. It was not an easy operation, however, as he was plagued by mosquitoes, spiders (with which he says he has "serious issues"), and underground rocks while he dug the hole, which took him 5 hours.

In September 2010, Breivik says: "I now have to acquire a semi-automatic rifle and Glock [pistol] legally... I don't have a criminal record so there is no reason why the police should reject my application." He goes on: "I have now sent an application for a Ruger Mini 14 semi-automatic rifle (5.56)... On the application form I stated: 'hunting deer.' It would have been tempting to just write the truth; 'executing category A and B cultural Marxists/multiculturalist traitors' just to see their reaction :P."

He goes on to say:

So what do I do when I'm not working? I'm in the middle of another steroid cycle at the moment, training hard to exceed my 92 kg record from July... I have a more or less perfect body at the moment and I'm as happy as I have ever been. My morale is at an all time high and I'm generally happy with how things are progressing. I may create an ideological Knights Templar YouTube movie this winter.

A video entitled *Knights Templar 2083* and posted on YouTube has been attributed to Breivik.

Later in the same entry:

As for girlfriends; I do get the occasional lead, or the occasional girl making a move, especially now a day as I'm fit like hell and feel great. But I'm trying to avoid relationships as it would only complicate my plans and it may jeopardize my operation.

In October–November 2010, he writes:

I have now made my first order for one of the chemicals required for my initiator from an online-based Polish supplier. I will have to order another 4-5 different ingredients online before I am done. Needless to say; this is an extremely vulnerable phase. In fact, it is the most vulnerable phase of them all. If I get through this phase without trouble I will be very close to finalizing my operation.

I am somewhat concerned but I have credible cover stories for each individual chemical (with the exception of one) should there be any complication.

Fears of detection are described repeatedly in the log.

Breivik details his calculations of operational discovery if future attackers do not want to get caught[2]:

All Justiciar Knights must ask themselves; should I manufacture explosives or just stick to fire arms? This decision really boils down to what you expect to accomplish. A well planned assault with an assault rifle may kill 30 category B traitors, while an unsuccessful explosive manufacturing process might result in 1 dead Justiciar Knight and thus 0 traitor executions. Also, there is a 30% chance of being

---

[2] *2083: A European Declaration of Independence.*

*apprehended during an explosive manufacturing
process (for a non-blacklisted person with no criminal
record) which doubles for every person involved. For
a blacklisted individual (blacklisted by the
intelligence agency) there is less than 10% chance for
success with the manufacture of explosives. If he
includes 3 other blacklisted individuals this 10%
chance is reduces to 3%.*

Part of the tract details his "personal reflections and experiences during several preparation phases," apparently in the run-up to the July 22 attacks.

Over dozens of pages, Breivik details his efforts meticulously to create cover stories for his plot, to build up his personal fitness levels, and to acquire the weaponry and explosive materials needed. It also sketches out aspects of his mental preparation for the act he intends to commit.

However, according to the Norwegian anti-Islamic citizen journalist website to which Breivik himself was a frequent contributor, large parts of the manifesto are copied directly from "Unabomber" Ted Kaczynski's own manifesto, with minor changes, such as replacement of the word "leftist" by the phrase "cultural Marxist."

The manifesto begins with an entry for April/May 2002, in which the author claims to have been "ordinated as the 8th Justiciar Knight for the PCCTS, Knights Templar Europe"—the "resistance movement" that elsewhere he claims has been established to combat the "Islamisation" of Europe:

*I joined the session after visiting one of the initial
facilitators, a Serbian Crusader Commander and war
hero, in Monrovia, Liberia... Our primary objective is
to develop PCCTS, Knights Templar into becoming*

the foremost conservative revolutionary movement in
Western Europe [in] the next few decades.

From 2002 to 2006, the log claims, Breivik raised funds for his venture—with 2006–2008 spent researching and writing his manifesto. By the autumn of 2009, the author claimed to be preparing for the next phase:

> I'm creating two different and "professional looking" prospectuses for "business ventures." A mining company and a small farm operation. The reasoning for this decision is to create a credible cover in case I am arrested in regards to the purchase and smuggling of explosives or components to explosives fertiliser. In this regard I created a new company called Geofarm, which might act as a credible cover for such activities.

Geofarm is a farm that has been linked to Anders Behring Breivik.

Breivik speaking about surveillance,[3] "the subject says that he, for the last three years—2009, 2010, and 2011—was afraid he was wiretapped." He says:

> There are many different lists for monitoring. I was looking for a way to verify whether I was on such a list. Thought I could already be on the watch list of a European intelligence agency. So I regarded it as a test when I was buying weapons, then it was unlikely that I was on watch lists anyway. But as long as it did not cost anything, I just as well took out the cell phone battery.

The subject says that he also took the battery out of his cell phone during a visit to Prague in 2010. "I was good at hiding clues," he said. When asked, he explains that he took the battery out of

---

[3] Court psychiatric report issued on November 29, 2011 to the Oslo District Court.

the phone both to "avoid being registered on the base stations, and to avoid wiretapping. In general, the last year I tried to leave the phone at home. I also used technology to hide my IP address."

The subject says he has been thinking a lot about wiretapping the last couple of years. "I took my precautions," he says, "but did not see any certain indications before June 18, 2011. Then I put together a number of factors."

The incident happened while the subject lived on his farm in Åsterdalen:

> That day I realized I was being watched. First I saw a police patrol by the road, then I saw a car with an extra antenna, and I had the feeling it was a civilian police car. It was suspiciously parked, 17 kilometers from the farm.

"Now the PST is on my farm installing cameras," the subject thought at that time. "It was unlikely to be local police, since they had a civilian police car. They were parked next to a bus stop and there were two men in the front seats."

"When I got home, the barn door was left wide open" and the subject thought "there still might be someone inside the house." He waited for 20 minutes, and says: "I thought about fighting my way to the Glock and then keep fighting. But I thought it was too much opposition, and that it was better to surrender without a fight."

It appears that the subject on this day was sure that surveillance cameras had been installed on the farm. He went searching for cameras inside the house when he got home. He says:

> *Checked for cameras on all potential places. They have stopped using microphones now, they use tiny cameras instead. I checked all the cracks and all the holes, natural places, but I found nothing. I thought it would be rational for them to install cameras, as they did with Al Qaeda. Plenty of evidence there.*

The subject says he has had thoughts about surveillance by cameras since February 2010. At that point, he considered getting detection equipment to find any cameras, but ended up searching carefully around him.

In the period from February 2010 to July 2010, the subject went into what he calls "the armor phase." He says: "I made a prototype body armor for a potential battle with Delta" (police special unit, experts' note). "I bought a box and put in it four bulletproof vest inserts, a pair of self-made bullet-proof pants, a bulletproof vest, and bulletproof shoes. And then I added smoke grenades and other things into the box, and drove to the Swedish border."

The subject explains how he found a deserted dirt road near Kongsvinger, and buried the box "next to a mosquito pond, so hunting dogs could not find it. Hunting dogs are in fact bothered by mosquitoes," he adds. The subject says he spent a whole day digging and made a hole a meter and a half deep. He put the box in it and camouflaged it with a rotten tree root on top. He says: "It was terribly hard work, but I made it."

As was highlighted before, it seems clear that Breivik was eager to paint himself as a lone warrior who was a single sleeper cell that was self-indoctrinated and planned over a period of 9 years with minimal interaction with others. His own account of obtaining equipment suggests he did this by himself with no outside support. He was also meticulous in building cover stories for himself prior to purchasing items that are available commonly but could raise suspicions if bought abruptly and in large quantities. From an ideological standpoint, some key meetings seem to have helped form his worldview, specifically his meeting in London in April 2002, although a number of key interactions appear to have taken place online as well.

In the last part of the compendium's diary entries, the subject described a history of gold mining in Finnmark on July 21 and 22, 2011. This he describes as the *remnant of a cover story* he had written into the manifest in case he was caught before the criminal acts. He did not have time, or in his own words he forgot, to remove the notes before the manifest was distributed. Quote:

Thursday July 21—Day 81: Drive 11 hours straight to Kautokeino, sort out cheap hotel.

Friday July 22—Day 82: Initiate blasting sequences at pre-determined sites. Test dirt for gram of gold per kg. Have enough material for at least 20 blasts. Start capitalization of project as soon as I have results. Time is running out, liquidity squeeze inc. Call/email all my investor contacts with updated online prospectus/pdf.

This is going to be an all-or-nothing scenario. If I fail to generate acceptable precious metals yields, in combination with swift initiation of the capitalization for securing the areas I will be heavily indebted. I must complete capitalization of the mineral extraction project within August at latest!

Figure 3.20 Anders Behring Breivik in custody immediately following his rampage.

When I have the required seed capital I will have enough funds to employ the services of professional blasting engineers.

If all fails, I will initiate my career with a private security firm in conflict zones to acquire maximum funds in the shortest period of time to repay the debts.

First coming costume party this autumn, dress up as a police officer. Arrive with insignias :-) Will be awesome as people will be very astonished :-)

Side note; imagine if law enforcement would visit me the next days. They would probably get the wrong idea and think I was a terrorist (Figure 3.20).

London Tube[4]

In July 2008, an Algerian national was stopped by two alert police officers who saw him using his cell phone camera to record video inside Liverpool Street Station in London (Figure 3.21). When the police officers examined the footage

[4] OSAC January 5, 2011, *Trends and Tactics: Case Study on Cell Phone Video Surveillance.*

*(U) CCTV footage catches police officers
walking toward the subject.*

Figure 3.21 CCTV footage catches police officers walking toward the subject.

they found 90 minutes of video recording of various sites in and around London and several U.K. cities, including tube and mainline rail stations, shopping areas, bars, and restaurants. His detention and the follow-up investigation led to the arrest of the subject's brother and a third Algerian male. British authorities also looked at 30 other individuals and recovered extremist material supporting al-Qa'ida in the Islamic Maghreb in one residence. Police believe the two brothers may have been fundraising and conducting surveillance for a future terrorist operation.

On July 11, 2008, the hostile surveillant entered Liverpool Street Station, a major London transit and retail hub. Liverpool Street Station is the third busiest station in London after Waterloo and Victoria stations. During peak hours, approximately 26,000 people per hour move through the main concourse area and an additional 100 trains an hour travel through the underground station, transporting another

30,000 people. At 11:15 AM, police officers noticed Subject 1 walking along the upper concourse filming and capturing all areas of the station. His behavior was deemed suspicious by the officers because he appeared to be covering the red light on his cell phone with his finger, indicating the phone was on video mode. The police stopped the surveillant and asked to see the footage on his cell phone. An examination of the phone revealed 90 minutes of film footage, including a series of 25-minute videos of various train/railroad stations, security cameras, entrances/exits, bars, restaurants, and shopping centers. The surveillant indicated he was a tourist and did not speak English. The police deemed both the video recording and the subject's interaction with them as suspicious. He was arrested under immigration offenses and transported to Bishops Gate police station. After reviewing the film footage further, authorities arrested Subject 1 under authority of the Terrorism Act of 2000.

Further investigation discovered that the surveillant arrived in Britain approximately 10 years prior; his brother arrived in the United Kingdom in 1997. Once in the United Kingdom, both men obtained national insurance numbers and took blue collar jobs in the service sector. They maintained a low-profile, living very simply in a one-room apartment in the London borough of Brent with the third Algerian. Having established themselves, they became involved in large-scale credit card and identity theft fraud, obtaining multiple credit cards on bogus applications, which they used to buy luxury goods to export to Algeria. The subjects also bought £5000 worth of cell phones with fraudulent credit cards.

According to a detective chief inspector involved in the case, "Extremist material suggesting a link to al- Qa'ida in North Africa was found during the search of one property...but he added that no connection was found between the Algerians and any known terrorist group in the United Kingdom." In addition to being involved in large-scale fraud, police believe that before going back to Algeria, the brothers carried out surveillance for a future terrorist attack.

"There are cameras, there are cameras everywhere." Voice of Subject 1 while filming Liverpool Station, July 7, 2008.

The investigation further revealed that the surveillant conducted extensive video surveillance from July 7 to 11. Although July 7 was the anniversary of the July 7, 2005 terror attacks in London, there is no indication that this was anything more than a coincidence. The video footage included the concourse at Liverpool Street Station, the nearby Broadgate Circle

(U) Entrance to Mornington Crescent Underground.

Figure 3.22 Video still from surveillant of entrance to Mornington Crescent Underground.

shopping and restaurant plaza, Mornington Crescent (one of the deepest stations on the tube network), and the Northern Line platforms at Camden town station (Figure 3.22).

He also took a tour bus ride through central London, getting off at the Oxford Circuit Underground Station. He filmed the foyer area of the station in which approximately 230,000 people travel through every day. Film footage also showed the brothers visiting the Galleria shopping centers in Hatfield and Bluewater, the Ashford shopping centers in Kent, and a trade outlet in Bridgend, South Wales. It is not known if their visit to the shopping centers was to conduct preoperational surveillance, make fraudulent credit card purchases, or both.

Although the surveillant did a significant amount of travel on the London tube and bus network during the cited period, police were unable to track him via his "oyster card" (electronic ticketing used on public transportation services in the greater London area of the United Kingdom). It is believed that the oyster cards were being swapped among multiple users to frustrate any subsequent CCTV research carried out by police.

Other indicators of surveillance tradecraft include conspicuously covering the red light on his mobile phone when video recording in the presence of others. When visiting various Tube and mainline stations, he concentrated on filming maps, trains, entrances/exits, and CCTV cameras. Throughout the film footage, he focused the camera on himself periodically. In these segments, he appears secretive and nervous, which are not synonymous with tourist photography. The reasons he did this were to (a) prove to others that it was him conducting the surveillance; (b) avoid unwanted attention from the public; and (c) capture footage from various angles, such as location of CCTV cameras on the ceilings of the stations. Of particular interest is when he turns the camera on its side to almost 90 degrees for no reason. This could signify the beginning and/or end of surveillance or highlight a specific target or targets. Interestingly, this was also done by al-Qa'ida operative Dhiren Barot while conducting video surveillance of the World Trade Center in New York City prior to the 9/11 attacks.

The surveillant is also periodically overheard making comments while video recording security countermeasures at some of the sites he visited. Around midnight on July 10, the day before his arrest, he visited Mornington Crescent, which is a "deep hole" Tube station only accessible by elevator. Inside the elevator, he is heard making comments about the location of CCTV cameras. After taking video footage of the CCTV cameras in the elevator, he turns the camera 90 degrees on its side (Figure 3.23).

In 2001, al-Qa'ida operative L'Hoyssaine Kherchtou testified in New York City that he took a 2-week surveillance seminar in a training camp in Pakistan in 1992. When asked if he trained in any particular equipment to use during surveillance, he replied, "Yes. We were trained how to use different cameras, especially small ones, develop the pictures, and to take the pictures holding the camera so that the surveillant is not looking through it."

(U) Footage of the security cameras inside an elevator (Mornington), then turning his camera 90 degrees on its side.

Figure 3.23 Captured surveillant footage of the security cameras inside an elevator, then turning the camera 90 degrees on its side.

7/7 London Attacks

The July 7, 2005 London bombings (often referred to as 7/7) were a series of coordinated suicide attacks in London, England that targeted civilians using the public transport system during the morning rush hour. On this routine Thursday morning, four Islamist home-grown terrorists detonated four bombs, three in quick succession aboard London Underground trains across the city and, later, a fourth on a double-decker bus in Tavistock Square (Figure 3.24). Fifty-two civilians and the four bombers were killed in the attacks, with over 700 more injured. The explosions were

Figure 3.24 The four London bombers captured on closed-circuit television. From left to right, Hasib Hussain, Germaine Lindsay, Mohammad Sidique Khan, and Shehzad Tanweer, pictured in the Luton train station at 07:21 AM, Thursday, July 7, 2005. Source: Scotland Yard.

caused by homemade organic peroxide-based devices packed into backpacks.

The four suicide bombers were later identified and named as

- Mohammad Sidique Khan: aged 30. Khan detonated his bomb just after leaving Edgware Road tube station on a train traveling toward Paddington at 8:50 am. He lived in Beeston, Leeds, with his wife and young child, where he worked as a learning mentor at a primary school. The blast killed seven people, including Khan himself.
- Shehzad Tanweer: aged 22. He detonated a bomb aboard a train traveling between Liverpool Street station and Aldgate tube station at 8:50 am. He lived in Leeds with his mother and father, working in a fish and chip shop. He was killed by the explosion along with seven members of the public.

- Germaine Lindsay: aged 19. He detonated his device on a train traveling between King's Cross and Russell Square tube stations at 8:50 am. He lived in Aylesbury, Buckinghamshire, with his pregnant wife and young son. His blast killed 27 people, including Lindsay himself.
- Hasib Hussain: the youngest of the four at 18, Hussain detonated his bomb on the top deck of a double-decker bus at 9:47 am. He lived in Leeds with his brother and sister-in-law. Fourteen people, including Hussain, died in the explosion in Tavistock Square.

Three of the bombers were British-born sons of Pakistani immigrants; Lindsay was a convert born in Jamaica.

10/20/74 Mohammad Sidique Khan (MSK) born in West Yorkshire:
- Attends local schools
- Works in local benefits agency and the department of trade and industry
- Goes on to study at Leeds Metropolitan University

12/15/82 Shehzad Tanweer (ST) born in West Yorkshire:
- Attends local schools
- Goes on to study at Leeds Metropolitan University
- Works in the family fish and chips shop

09/23/85 Germaine Lindsay (GL) born in Jamaica:
- Moves to the United Kingdom with his mother in 1986
- Attends local schools in home town of Huddersfield
- Works occasional odd jobs

09/16/86 Hasib Hussain (HH) born in West Yorkshire:

* Attends local schools
* Goes on to college to study an advanced business program

Late 1990s MSK: Starts youth work.

2000 GL: Following mother's conversion, converts to Islam and takes the name Jamal.

2001 MSK: Joins staff of local primary school to work as a learning mentor.

October 2001 MSK: Marries. Later moves to Batley and then Dewsbury.

Mid-2002 ST: Religion appears to become the main focus of his life.

2002 HH: Makes Hajj visit to Saudi Arabia and to family in Pakistan. Returns to England. Increasingly religiously observant.

October 2002 GL: Marries, lives in Huddersfield.

Early 2003 MSK and ST: Become increasingly close.

Early 2003 MSK: Hajj visit with his wife.

April 2003 MSK and ST: Camping trip in the United Kingdom with other young men.

July 2003 MSK: Visits Pakistan for training.

September 2003 GL: Moves to Aylesbury.

April 2004 GL: First child born. Works as a carpet fitter until early 2005.

ST: Caution for disorderly conduct.

May 2004 MSK: Daughter born.

October 2004 HH: Cautioned for shoplifting.

Late 2004 MSK and GL: Close association.

September–November 2004 MSK: Long period of sick absence from work. Job ends.

November–February 2005 MSK and ST: Visit Pakistan.

Mar 2005: First purchase of material to make explosives.

Figure 3.25 Entering Luton station on what is believed was a reconnaissance trip: Mohammad Sidique Khan, in white hat, Germaine Lindsay, in black hat, and Shehzad Tanweer (Metropolitan Police, via Associated Press).

May 2005 GL: Rents Alexandra Grove, the bomb factory.
June 2005 MSK and ST: White-water rafting trip with other young men.
June 28, 2005 MSK, ST, and GL: recce visit to London[5] (Figures 3.25–3.28).

What happened in London on 7 July 2005 could happen at any time, in any city, in any country.

London Resilience/Metropolitan Police Service training video

---

[5] Report of the official account of the bombings in London on 7th July 2005, 2006.

Figure 3.26 A surveillance photo of Shehzad Tanweer (second to the left), Mohammad Sidique Khan (far right), and Omar Khyam (center) taken in a parking lot of a McDonald's restaurant on February 28, 2004. Source: Metropolitan Police.

Figure 3.27 Mohammad Sidique Khan (left) and Shehzad Tanweer (right) passing through immigration control in Karachi, Pakistan. Source: Public domain.

3.2.2 Domestic Terrorist (U.S.)

3.2.2.1 Amateurs, Wannabes, and Lone Wolves

Fort Dix Six

The case of the Fort Dix Six is a victory for citizen reporting and should be heralded by the DHS when discussing the "See Something, Say Something" campaign as an example of why it is important to report something suspicious (Figure 3.29).

Figure 3.28 Shehzad Tanweer in his last testament video.
Source: Agence France-Presse.

In 2007, a teenage clerk at Circuit City in Mount Laurel, New Jersey, was asked by two men to transfer a videotape to a digital video disk (DVD). When the teenager and another

Figure 3.29 Joint Base McGuire-Dix-Lakehurst, is a former United States Army post located approximately 16 miles south-southeast of Trenton, New Jersey.

Figure 3.30 Fort Dix Six terrorist tipster Brian Morganstern.

employee went into the back room and started the process of transferring the tape, they found themselves watching several men in "fundamentalist attire" and shooting "big, f-ing guns," the teen later told co-workers. The teen frantically told his co-worker what he had witnessed. And then he said, "I don't know what to do. Should I call someone or is that being racist"[6] (Figure 3.30)?

Sixteen months after the teenage clerk reported the video, the FBI arrested a group of terrorists that became known as the "Fort Dix Six." At the time the FBI believed the "Fort Dix Six" were finalizing their plans for an assault on Fort Dix. The group was convicted on December 22, 2008 (Figure 3.31).

[6] Jana Winter, "Clerk Rings up N.J. Jihad Clerks," *New York Post*, May 13, 2007.

Figure 3.31 Members of "Fort Dix Six."

Figure 3.32 Defendants of "Fort Dix Six."

The defendants and the charges on which each was convicted are as follow (Figures 3.32 and 3.33).

- Mohamad Ibrahim Shnewer, 23, of Cherry Hill: conspiracy to murder members of the

Figure 3.33 *New York Post* headline.

U.S. military and attempted possession of AK-47 semiautomatic assault weapons to be used in the attack.

- Dritan Duka, 30, of Cherry Hill: conspiracy to murder members of the U.S. military, possession of machine guns, possession and attempted possession of machine guns in furtherance of a crime of violence, and two counts of possession of firearms by an illegal alien.
- Shain Duka, 27, of Cherry Hill: conspiracy to murder members of the U.S. military, possession of machine guns, possession and attempted possession of machine guns in furtherance of a crime of violence, and two counts of possession of firearms by an illegal alien.
- Eljvir Duka, 25, of Cherry Hill: conspiracy to murder members of the U.S. military and possession of firearms by an illegal alien. The jury acquitted on one count of possession

and attempted possession of machine guns in furtherance of a crime of violence.

- Serdar Tatar, 25, of Philadelphia: conspiracy to murder members of the U.S. military.

From the U.S. District Court District of New Jersey Criminal Complaint,[7] one can readily review the number of preattack activities and preoperational surveillance activities that occurred.

OVERT ACTS

In furtherance of the conspiracy and to effect the objects thereof, defendant ELJVIR DUKA, aka "Elvis Duka," aka "Sulayman," and others committed and caused to be committed overt acts in the District of New Jersey, and elsewhere, including but not limited to:

a. On or about January 3, 2006, MOHAMAD SHNEWER, DRITAN DUKA, ELJVIR DUKA, SHAIN DUKA, and SERDAR TATAR conducted firearms training in Gouldsboro, Pennsylvania.

b. On or about August 11, 2006, MOHAMAD SHNEWER traveled to the United States Army base at Fort Dix, New Jersey to conduct surveillance.

c. On or about August 11, 2006, MOHAMAD SHNEWER traveled to the United States Army base at Fort Monmouth, New Jersey to conduct surveillance.

d. On or about August 13, 2006, MOHAMAD SHNEWER traveled to Dover Air Force base in Dover, Delaware to conduct surveillance.

e. On or about August 13, 2006, MOHAMAD SHNEWER traveled to the United States Coast Guard Building in Philadelphia, Pennsylvania to conduct surveillance.

f. On or about November 28, 2006, SERDAR TATAR acquired a map of the United States Army base at Fort Dix, New Jersey, labeled "Cantonment Area Fort Dix, NJ" to be distributed to others.

g. On or about January 31, 2007, DRITAN DUKA, ELJVIR DUKA, and SHAINDUKA collected weapons, including hand guns, shotguns, and semiautomatic assault weapons to be used in small arms training.

[7] Magistrate No. 07-M-2047 (JS).

h. On or about February 1, 2007, DRITAN DUKA, ELJVIR DUKA, and SHAINDUKA traveled by car from New Jersey to Pennsylvania in order to conduct firearms training.

i. On or about February 2, 2007, DRITAN DUKA, SHAIN DUKA, and ELJVIRDUKA conducted firearms training in Gouldsboro, Pennsylvania.

j. On or about February 4, 2007, MOHAMAD SHNEWER, DRITAN DUKA, ELJVIR DUKA, and SHAIN DUKA reviewed terrorist training videos.

k. On or about February 26, 2007, DRITAN DUKA and ELJVIR DUKA conducted tactical training in Cherry Hill, New Jersey.

l. On or about March 15, 2007, DRITAN DUKA and SHAIN DUKA conducted tactical training in Cherry Hill, New Jersey.

m. On or about April 6, 2007, DRITAN DUKA ordered four AK-47 Kalishnikov fully automatic machine guns as well as M-16 firearms and handguns.

n. On or about April 27, 2007, MOHAMAD SHNEWER ordered an AK-47 Kalishnikov fully automatic machine gun.

On or about January 31, 2006, a representative of a retail store informed officials of the FBI that an individual had brought a video to their store to be duplicated onto a DVD. That DVD depicted conduct—recorded as having occurred on January 3, 2006—that the store representative described as disturbing. FBI agents reviewed the DVD in question. The DVD depicted 10 young men who appeared to be in their early twenties shooting assault weapons at a firing range in a militia-like style while calling for *jihad* and shouting in Arabic "Allah Akbar" ("God is great"). The FBI and Joint Terrorism Task Force (JTTF) immediately commenced an investigation into the activities of the men depicted in the DVD (Figure 3.34).

The FBI identified the 10 men depicted in the DVD, six of whom are Mohamad Shnewer, Dritan Duka, aka "Distan Duka," aka "Anthony

Figure 3.34 Some of the men depicted in the DVD.

Duka," aka "Tony Duka," Eljvir Duka, aka "Elvis Duka," aka "Sulayman," Shain Duka, Serdar Tatar, and Agron Abdullahu. Immigration and customs enforcement checks showed that Dritan Duka, Eljvir Duka, and Shain Duka were residing in the United States illegally.

In or about March 2006, a cooperating witness ("CW-1") infiltrated this group successfully by developing a relationship with Mohamad Shnewer. Beginning in or about March 2006, CW-1 consensually recorded conversations with Shnewer and other targets of the investigation during meetings and telephone calls.

On or about April 14, 2006, CW-1 consensually recorded a meeting with Mohamad Shnewer. During that meeting, Shnewer stated that he and CW-1 should view a video stored on

Shnewer's computer, but that they had to do so in private because "it's about something that can lead to prison."

On or about April 28, 2006, during a consensually recorded meeting with CW-1, Mohamad Shnewer downloaded a DVD from his laptop computer, which Shnewer then provided to CW-1. Shnewer instructed CW-1 to review the DVD alone. CW-1 provided the DVD to FBI and JTTF agents, who reviewed the DVD. The DVD contained video footage of various jihadist images while a narrator recruited the observer to the jihadist movement.

On or about May 26, 2006, during a consensually recorded meeting with CW-1, Mohamad Shnewer gave CW-1 Shnewer's laptop computer and told CW-1 to review particular DVD files on the laptop hard drive. CW-1 asked Shnewer to write the names of the DVD files Shnewer wanted CW-1 to review, which Shnewer did.

CW-1 provided a business card to FBI and JTTF agents on which Shnewer had written the names of the DVD files CW-1 was to review. One file was named "19" and the other file was named "VTS_01_1." Law enforcement officials made a copy of Shnewer's laptop hard drive and were able to locate and view the files labeled "19" and "VTS_01_1." The file labeled "19" contained what appears to be the last will and testament of at least two of the highjackers involved in the terrorist attacks on the United States on September 11, 2001.

The file labeled "VTS_01_1" contained images of Osama Bin Laden and other Islamic extremists making various speeches in which the speakers call the viewer to join the jihadist movement.

On or about July 7, 2006, a second individual who was cooperating with the FBI ("CW-2") was approached by six males unknown to CW-2. One of the males identified himself as "Sulayman" and invited CW-2 to his home. The investigation revealed that Eljvir Duka uses the name "Sulayman."

On or about July 28, 2006, CW-1 consensually recorded a meeting with Serdar Tatar during which Tatar asked CW-1 to fix Tatar's vehicle. CW-1 and Tatar then switched vehicles. CW-1 delivered Tatar's vehicle to law enforcement officers. CW-1 consented to a search of the vehicle. Inside the vehicle, law enforcement officers found a 50-round box of 9-mm ammunition. On the same day, CW-2 consensually recorded a meeting with Dritan Duka, Eljvir Duka, and Shain Duka. Eljvir Duka told CW-2 that the Dukas go target shooting with firearms but cannot go to regular gun ranges because none of them are legal residents of the United States. Dritan Duka showed CW-2 a video on Dritan Duka's cell phone that depicted individuals shooting firearms. Dritan Duka stated that this activity took place in Pennsylvania. CW-2 informed law enforcement agents that during the meeting, CW-2 learned that the Duka brothers keep their firearms with Eljvir Duka's brother-in-law, an individual named "Agim," and an individual named "Mohamad." Law enforcement officials determined that Eljvir Duka's brother-in-law is Mohamad Shnewer and that the individual named "Agim" is Agron Abdullahu.

On or about July 29, 2006, CW-2 consensually recorded a meeting with Mohamad Shnewer, Dritan Duka, Eljvir Duka, and Shain Duka. During the meeting, Shnewer showed CW-2 a number of videos on Shnewer's laptop computer that depicted armed attacks on and the killing of U.S. military personnel. CW-2 observed that Shnewer seemed to enjoy watching the video and smiled during the viewing.

On or about August 1, 2, and 5, 2006, CW-1 consensually recorded meetings with Mohamad Shnewer. In summary, Shnewer stated that he, Serdar Tatar, Dritan Duka, Eljvir Duka, Shain Duka, and others were part of a group that was planning to attack a U.S. military base. Shnewer specifically named the U.S. Army base at Fort Dix, New Jersey, and a nearby U.S. Navy base. Shnewer explained that they could utilize six or seven jihadists to attack and kill at least 100 soldiers by using rocket-propelled grenades (RPGs) or other weapons. Shnewer further explained that they could train for the attack in Pennsylvania. Shnewer also said that he and others in the group had saved money to pay for the weapons and that they were not afraid to die. Shnewer stated further that Tatar could obtain maps of Fort Dix in order to plan the attack. Shnewer also said that the group wanted CW-1 to help lead the attack based on CW-1's prior experience in the Egyptian military.

On August 1, 2006, Mohamad Shnewer said the following, in substance and in part:

If you want to do anything here, there is Fort Dix and I don't want to exaggerate, and I assure you that you can hit an American base very easily. You take a map and draw it and then you calculate that there are areas where there are 100–200 individuals and you should allocate 6–7 persons for this alone. When you go to a military base, you need mortars and RPGs. . . . I am at your services as you have more experience than me in military bases and in life.

On August 2, 2006, Mohamad Shnewer said the following, in substance and in part:

There is a nice area where we can train . . . In Pennsylvania . . . It is two hours away from here. Don't worry about money. I have money too as I have been saving money for this plan for some time. Both Sulayman and Tony [meaning Eljvir Duka and Dritan Duka] have a lot of money.

In response to how the group would get a map of Fort Dix, Shnewer said the following: "Serdar, he used to deliver there... Why did I choose Fort Dix? Because I know that Serdar knows it like the palm of his hand"[8] (Figure 3.35).

On August 5, 2006, Mohamad Shnewer said the following, in substance and in part.

Figure 3.35 Serdar Tatar's family pizzeria near Fort Dix.

[8] Subsequent consensually recorded conversations revealed that Serdar Tatar used to deliver pizzas to Fort Dix. Law enforcement officers verified that Tatar's family owns a pizzeria near Fort Dix.

In response to CW-1's question regarding who Shnewer had in mind for the attack:

I have in mind Tony [meaning Dritan/Duka], Sulayman [meaning Eljvir Duka], Shaheen [meaning Shain Duka]...Serdar, definitely, he is the first one amongst us...

Concerning training:

You are in the mountains in the Poconos...In Pennsylvania. It is about two hours away from here. We went there for a week walking in the mountains and shooting in the open shooting range. We need to accumulate experience, and we need to think about how many we need and what they are going to do and we need to gather the weapons...Of course, I can get the weapons, machine gun, hand gun, I can get... from the street as you cannot buy a machine gun from a store.

In response to whether Shnewer had spoken with Eljvir Duka or Dritan Duka about being part of the group:

"I spoke with them some time ago, and they are ready. All the names I mentioned are ready and on alert, specifically the four brothers and Serdar, that means Tony, Sulayman..."

During the consensually recorded meeting on August 5, 2006, Mohamad Shnewer also suggested that he and CW-1 surveil military bases to decide which one to attack. When discussing the naval base, Shnewer said,

Maybe it is easy to hit them, there are nights where the squad is out and doing exercises without weapons... the only problem is that they may have protection and scouts watching. You know what we can do is go one day to a nearby restaurant and observe the whole base.

When CW-1 asked whether they could take pictures during their surveillance, Shnewer said that doing so would be very dangerous but that they could film the base using a cell phone camera:

> Same thing for Fort Dix, you cannot take pictures as it is very difficult to do so. You know what, we can take pictures by using the phone and you make as if you are talking on the cell phone and you will take a video . . . In Fort Dix, yeah, while you are driving, we will drive slow and what is nice with the phone is that if you are stopped by a police, you will delete it from memory.

On or about August 11, 2006, CW-1 and Mohamad Shnewer traveled to the Fort Dix military base to conduct surveillance. CW-1 consensually recorded the trip. While Shnewer and CW-1 were driving to Fort Dix, Shnewer spoke with another person on the telephone—captured on the consensually monitored recording—during which Shnewer asked the individual what street the person's pizzeria was on. Shnewer also said that Shnewer, Eljvir Duka, Dritan Duka, Shain Duka, Serdar Tatar, and CW-1 were part of the group that would attack the military base. When CW-1 asked what made Shnewer think of Fort Dix as a target, Shnewer replied, "My intent is to hit a heavy concentration of soldiers...." As Shnewer and CW-1 drove into a specific area at Fort Dix, Shnewer said, " ...this is exactly what we are looking for. You hit 4, 5, or 6 humvees and light the whole place [up] and retreat completely without any losses." Shnewer and CW-1 then drove to Lakehurst Naval Air Station. On the way there, Shnewer remarked that "this is going to be easier to hit specially if you have 8 or 9 shooting with machine guns and they are good shooters."

Figure 3.36 The U.S. Army base at Fort Monmouth, New Jersey.

During the surveillance trip, Shnewer received several telephone calls and lied about his whereabouts to the callers.

After Mohamad Shnewer and CW-1 completed the surveillance trip, law enforcement officers observed Shnewer later that evening driving by himself to the U.S. Army base at Fort Monmouth, New Jersey (Figure 3.36).

On or about August 13, 2006, during the evening hours, Mohamad Shnewer called CW-1 (Figure 3.37). CW-1 recorded the conversation. During the conversation, Shnewer asked CW-1 to go with him to surveil the Dover Air Force base in Dover, Delaware. CW-1 then met Shnewer and recorded their trip to the Dover Air Force Base. During the trip, Shnewer played a video on his computer that taught the viewer how to make a grenade. Shnewer said that

Figure 3.37 Mohammed Shnewer's home in Cherry Hill. Photograph: Matt Rourke/AP.

"Sulayman [Eljvir Duka]... told me that they have high security over there. You can see the planes taking off. Sometimes, there are 300 soldiers." Shnewer also explained that he had informed Eljvir Duka that he had gone to surveil Fort Dix. Shnewer further said that Eljvir Duka could get machine guns. Shnewer acknowledged that "in all of the U.S. it's illegal to sell on or about September 14, 2006." CW-1 consensually recorded a meeting with Mohamad Shnewer and Shain Duka. During this meeting, CW-1 asked Shain Duka to have Eljvir Duka call CW-1. Shnewer explained to Shain Duka, "We've been brain-storming, we were going to look at some areas... we got one, one idea for something and we wanted to know who's in, who's not." Shain Duka responded, "Alright." CW-1 then mentioned machine guns and Shain Duka responded, "Ah." When CW-1 mentioned that they could go to jail forever, Shain Duka responded, "Gotta be cautious." When CW-1 asked if Shain Duka was "with them," Shain Duka responded, "God willing, we will see."

On or about September 22, 2006 and September 29, 2006, CW-1 consensually recorded two meetings with Eljvir Duka. In summary, Eljvir Duka stated that they would need to receive a "fatwa" before they could attack.

On or about October 6, 2006, CW-2 attempted to consensually record a meeting with Dritan Duka, Shain Duka, and Mohamad Shnewer. The equipment, however, failed to record the meeting. CW-2 informed law enforcement officers that during the meeting, Shnewer told CW-2 that he had new videos for CW-2 to watch, one of which included training conducted by the attackers on September 11, 2001. CW-2 also informed law enforcement officers that Shain Duka mentioned planning a trip to the Poconos for a week so that the group could shoot firearms.

On or about October 31, 2006, CW-1 consensually recorded a meeting with Serdar Tatar during which CW-1 and Tatar discussed Fort Dix. When CW-1 expressed anger at the United States, Tatar stated in response, "You want to make them pay for something that they did . . . Okay, you need maps?" Tatar then told CW-1 that he would give CW-1 a map of Fort Dix.

On or about November 3, 2006, during a consensually recorded meeting, Mohamad Shnewer and CW-1 discussed Serdar Tatar providing a map of Fort Dix. Shnewer also said that individuals likely to attend another trip to the Poconos included Dritan Duka, Eljvir Duka, Shain Duka, Serdar Tatar, and Agron Abdullahu. When CW-1 mentioned that he might have a source who could supply firearms, Shnewer expressed interest.

On or about November 9, 2006, CW-1 consensually recorded a telephone conversation with Serdar Tatar during which Tatar indicated that he would provide the map of Fort Dix to CW-1 shortly.

On or about November 12, 2006, CW-1 consensually recorded a meeting with Serdar Tatar during which Tatar explained that he would acquire the map of Fort Dix from his father's restaurant. Tatar acknowledged that he was "in" the plan to attack Fort Dix, stating "I'm in, honestly I'm in." However, Tatar cautioned CW-1 that they, the group, needed to ensure that their families would be protected. Tatar described a place at Fort Dix they could target that would cause a power outage and allow for an easier attack on the military personnel there. At the very end of the meeting, Tatar questioned CW-1 about whether CW-1 was a "Fed"—meaning a law enforcement officer.

On or about November 13, 2006, CW-1 consensually recorded a telephone call with Mohamad Shnewer. Toward the end of the call, Shnewer said that he was coming to CW-1's residence. CW-1 then consensually recorded that meeting. During the meeting, Shnewer and CW-1 discussed Serdar Tatar acquiring the map of Fort Dix, machine guns, and the upcoming trip to the Poconos where the group would train. Shnewer also told CW-1 that he hid his firearms inside the air conditioning unit at his house. Shnewer reiterated that Shain Duka and Dritan Duka knew of the plan and would be participating.

On or about November 14, 2006, CW-1 consensually recorded a meeting with Eljvir

Duka during which CW-1 and Eljvir Duka discussed Serdar Tatar potentially acquiring a map of Fort Dix. When CW-1 repeated Tatar's concerns about the need to take care of family before the attacks, Eljvir Duka responded that "Allah" will take care of Tatar's family. CW-1 and Eljvir Duka also discussed the need to use coded language when discussing the upcoming trip to the Poconos.

In a possible effort to determine whether CW-1 was a law enforcement officer, on November 15, 2006, Serdar Tatar contacted a sergeant with the Philadelphia Police Department and stated that he had been approached by an individual who had pressured him to acquire maps of Fort Dix. Tatar also told the police officer that he did not supply the map and was fearful that the incident was terrorist related. The sergeant telephoned the FBI in Tatar's presence.

The next day, on November 16, 2006, Serdar Tatar told CW-1 during a consensually monitored telephone call that Serdar Tatar would supply CW-1 with a map of Fort Dix.

On or about November 27, 2006, CW-1 consensually recorded a telephone call with Serdar Tatar during which Tatar said that too many people were in the restaurant for Tatar to take the map of Fort Dix.

On or about November 28, 2006, CW-1 consensually recorded a meeting with Serdar Tatar. During the meeting, Tatar acknowledged that if he were to provide a map of Fort Dix he could be deported. Tatar also expressed his willingness to participate by providing the map, even in the face of significant consequences:

You know one thing that's scary too? . . . I don't know you that much . . . You know. I don't know whether you're FBI .. . or the, an agent, don't know." "I'm gonna do it. Whether you are or not (FBI) I'm gonna do it. Know why? . . . It doesn't matter to me, whether I get locked up, arrested, or get taken away, it doesn't matter. Or I die, doesn't matter, I'm doing it in the name of Allah.

Later in the evening of November 28, 2006, Serdar Tatar called CW-1 when CW-1 was not at home (a call, therefore, that was not recorded) and stated, in substance and in part, that Tatar had left a package for CW-1 at the guard shack outside of CW-1's residence. This call was unrecorded. CW-1 then called Tatar back from CW-1's residence while consensually recording the call. Tatar immediately asked CW-1, "You get it brother?" CW-1 then asked Tatar where Tatar had put the map. Tatar then described the location where he had hidden the map. After the call, CW-1 went to the location described by Tatar and found a map labeled "Cantonment Area Fort Dix, NJ" (Figure 3.38).

On or about November 29, 2006, CW-1 turned the map Serdar Tatar had provided over to law enforcement officers who made copies of it and returned the original to CW-1. Law enforcement officers also reviewed CW-1's call log on CW-1's cell phone and observed that CW-1 had received a telephone call at 10:51 PM on November 28, 2006 from telephone number 856-520-4291 that lasted approximately 2 minutes. Law enforcement officers determined that 856-520-4291 was Serdar Tatar's cell phone number.

Figure 3.38

On or about November 30, 2006, during a consensually recorded telephone call, CW-1 informed Mohamad Shnewer that Serdar Tatar had provided the map of Fort Dix. Shnewer stated that he would come see the map shortly.

On or about December 1, 2006, CW-2 consensually recorded a meeting with Shain Duka, Dritan Duka, and Eljvir Duka during which the firearms needed for the upcoming trip to the Poconos were discussed. Dritan Duka said the group had a shotgun and a .357 magnum firearm, which they had purchased on the black market. Shain Duka explained that they hid this weapon. Eljvir Duka said they also had a small automatic weapon.

On or about December 7, 2006, law enforcement officers with the FBI interviewed Serdar Tatar. Tatar provided his cell phone number as 856-520-4291—the same number law enforcement officers had observed previously on the call log of CW-1's cell phone. Tatar falsely told the interviewing officers that he was not a part of the plot to attack Fort Dix and did not know any of the parties that may be involved. Tatar denied falsely three times that he had provided a map of Fort Dix to anyone.

On or about December 8, 2006, during a consensually recorded meeting, Mohamad Shnewer confirmed that Serdar Tatar had told Shnewer that Tatar had given CW-1 the map of Fort Dix. Shnewer also stated that they had missed an opportunity to attack U.S. military personnel during the Army–Navy football game that had been played recently in Philadelphia.

On or about December 27, 2006, CW-1 consensually recorded a telephone call with Mohamad Shnewer during which Shnewer informed CW-1 that the trip to the Poconos was scheduled for February 1, 2007. Shnewer further stated that he would take the map of Fort Dix from CW-1.

On or about December 28, 2006, CW-1 consensually recorded a telephone call with Shain Duka and Eljvir Duka. During the call, Eljvir Duka told CW-1 that the Pocono trip was scheduled for February 1, 2007 and that they had already rented a house.

On or about December 29, 2006, CW-1 consensually recorded a meeting with Mohamad

Shnewer during which Shnewer reviewed the map of Fort Dix. Shnewer took the map from CW-1 and placed it in his mother's car. Later, when Eljvir Duka joined the meeting, CW-1 discussed Serdar Tatar providing the map of Fort Dix. After Eljvir Duka left the meeting, Shnewer told CW-1 that Eljvir Duka had said that Fort Dix was a good target. Shnewer also stated that he was setting money aside to buy a fully automatic machine gun from CW-1's source. Shnewer acknowledged the illegality of such a weapon, stating "it is forbidden to use fully automatic" and that the penalty was imprisonment.

On or about January 5, 2007, CW-2 consensually recorded a meeting with Eljvir Duka and Serdar Tatar during which Eljvir Duka discussed the upcoming Pocono trip and stated that it had been scheduled for February 1, 2007.

On or about January 7, 2007, during a consensually recorded telephone call with Mohamad Shnewer, CW-1 expressed concern that SHNEWER's mother might find the map of Fort Dix that Shnewer had placed earlier in his mother's car. Shnewer replied that he had hidden the map.

On or about January 16, 2007, CW-1 consensually recorded a telephone call with Mohamad Shnewer during which Shnewer made arrangements with CW-1 to travel to the Poconos.

On or about January 19, 2007, CW-2 consensually recorded a meeting with Eljvir Duka, Dritan Duka, and Shain Duka during which the Pocono trip and firearms were discussed. Dritan Duka explained that the group had four firearms. Eljvir Duka also said that they had a 9-mm handgun, an assault rifle, and a semi-automatic assault weapon. Dritan Duka explained that Agron Abdullahu brought the rifle and ammunition to them because he had a license for the weapon. Eljvir, Shain, and Dritan Duka all explained that they could not have firearms because they did not have "green cards." During the consensually recorded meeting, Shain Duka identified the individuals who would be going to the Poconos, which included Dritan Duka, Eljvir Duka, Shain Duka, CW-2, Agron Abdullahu, Shnewer, and CW-1. CW-2 was told that everyone would meet at Dritan Duka's house on January 31, 2007, sleep over, and then leave for the Poconos early the next morning.

Between January 31 and February 1, 2007, law enforcement officers conducted video and photographic surveillance of Dritan Duka's residence in Cherry Hill, New Jersey. Law enforcement officers observed Agron Abdullahu and Dritan Duka carrying dark-colored rifle-style bags into Dritan Duka's residence at separate times (Figure 3.39). CW-2 consensually recorded conversations at Dritan Duka's residence, during which Dritan brought out the firearms. The individuals were heard racking the action of the firearms. CW-2 subsequently informed law enforcement officers that CW-2 had observed two firearms on the floor by the fireplace in Dritan Duka's residence and had handled the weapons with Dritan Duka, Eljvir Duka, and Shain Duka. CW-2 also subsequently reported that Abdullahu had brought two fire-arms to Dritan Duka's residence—a 9-mm handgun and a Yugoslavian semiautomatic

Figure 3.39 Dark-colored rifle-style bag being carried into the residence of Dritan Duka.

rifle. Law enforcement officers observed Shain Duka carrying a green rifle-style soft case from Dritan Duka's residence to Abdullahu, who loaded it into Abdullahu's vehicle. CW-2 reported that Abdullahu placed the two firearms he had brought into Dritan Duka's residence into his vehicle to transport to the Poconos, along with a shotgun and a Beretta rifle that were also at Dritan Duka's residence. Law enforcement officers observed Dritan Duka, Eljvir Duka, Shain Duka, Agron Abdullahu, and others depart Dritan Duka's residence on February 1, 2007.

CW-2 traveled to 2717 Eagleview Drive, Gouldsboro, Pennsylvania on February 1, 2007 with Shain Duka, Eljvir Duka, Dritan Duka, Agron Abdullahu, and others—the location of

Figure 3.40 The house the Duka brothers rented for the Pocono trip.

the house the Duka brothers rented for the Pocono trip (Figure 3.40).

On or about February 2, 2007, CW-1 consensually recorded a telephone call with Mohamad Shnewer and the two made arrangements to travel to the Poconos 2 days later. On the same day, law enforcement officers conducted video surveillance at Pennsylvania State Game Land 127—the same firearms range captured on the January 3, 2006 DVD described previously—and observed Dritan Duka, Shain Duka, and Eljvir Duka all firing weapons from various positions. Law enforcement officers subsequently learned that these individuals were using an SKS semiautomatic rifle, a Beretta Storm semiautomatic rifle, a Mossberg 12-gauge pump shotgun, and a 9-mm Beretta handgun. Law enforcement officers observed Shain Duka directing all the participants as they were setting up their shooting stations. Law enforcement officers also observed Agron Abdullahu teaching several individuals where to place the shotgun when firing it. Law enforcement officers observed Dritan Duka watching all the participants as they were shooting.

On or about February 3, 2007, a surveillance camera at the firing range again captured Eljvir

Figure 3.41 A surveillance camera at the firing range capturing Eljvir Duka, Shain Duka, Dritan Duka, and others firing weapons.

Duka, Shain Duka, Dritan Duka, and others firing weapons (Figure 3.41). Earlier that day, an undercover FBI agent who had been conducting surveillance at the firearms range on February 2, 2007 unexpectedly encountered Eljvir Duka and Dritan Duka at a local convenience store. Dritan Duka engaged the undercover agent in a conversation. Eljvir Duka asked the undercover agent if he knew where Eljvir Duka and Dritan Duka could purchase AK-47 and M-16 firearms. Dritan Duka continued the conversation with the undercover agent and discussed that "they" wanted to buy the Russian version of the AK-47 instead of the cheaper Chinese version because of its durability and capability of being buried in dirt and sand. Dritan Duka also said that AK-47s were easier to purchase overseas, particularly in Lebanon. When the undercover agent asked what type of weapons Dritan Duka and his friends had been using that day at the range, Dritan Duka replied that they had been shooting a Beretta CX-4 9-mm rifle with a synthetic stock, a Beretta shotgun with a synthetic stock, "just like the cops use," and a Beretta semiautomatic nickel-plated handgun.

On or about February 4, 2007, CW-1 consensually recorded conversations undertaken during his trip to the Poconos with Mohamad Shnewer. On the way, Shnewer recounted the earlier trip he made to the Poconos and stated that the group had used five firearms and that each shooter had fired approximately 400 bullets. CW-1 also again expressed concern that someone might find the map of Fort Dix that Shnewer had taken from CW-1. Shnewer replied that he had hidden the map in a room in his house that no one else enters. At one point, Shnewer remarked that the acquisition of RPGs by the group would increase the number of killings the group could cause.

Mohamad Shnewer and CW-1 arrived at the rental house in the Poconos on or about February 4, 2007. CW-1 continued to consensually record once at the rental house (Figure 3.42). CW-1 captured Shnewer playing videos on his laptop computer, which members of the group referred to as Mujahideen and terrorist training

Figure 3.42 The group watching terrorist training videos on Shnewer's laptop computer.

videos. Members of the group pointed out that U.S. military vehicles were shown being destroyed in various attacks. Shain Duka pointed out that a U.S. Marine's arm had been blown off, at which point laughter erupted from the group. CW-2 subsequently reported to law enforcement officers that after Shnewer arrived, the group watched terrorist training videos on Shnewer's laptop computer.

In the early hours of February 5, 2007, while CW-1 was still consensually recording conversations involving the targets at the rental house, several members of the group engaged in a discussion concerning bombs, nitroglycerin, and the explosive C-4.

Later in the day, CW-1 consensually recorded the group shooting weapons. That afternoon, CW-1 and Mohamad Shnewer left the rental house and CW-1 consensually recorded the conversations that took place during their trip back to New Jersey. On the way, Shnewer again identified which members of the group would participate in the attacks on the U.S. military, namely, Shain Duka, Dritan Duka, Eljvir Duka, CW-1, himself, and a younger brother of the Dukas. Shnewer also said that they could attack two American warships next year when they docked in the Port of Philadelphia. In addition, Shnewer discussed the weapons the group would need, saying "[t]he machine gun, we are going to buy the machine gun, but we need other than the machine gun. Something else."

On or about February 8, 2007, CW-2 consensually recorded conversations during CW-2's return trip to New Jersey with Eljvir Duka and

Dritan Duka. During this trip, Eljvir Duka and Dritan Duka discussed the need to train so that they could go overseas on "jihad." Eljvir Duka indicated that the Pocono trip had been a training mission. He also stated: " . . .and at the end when it comes to defending your religion, when someone is trying attacks your religion, your way of life, then you go jihad."

On or about February 18, 2007, CW-1 consensually recorded a telephone conversation with Dritan Duka during which Dritan Duka and CW-1 discussed "training" by playing paint ball with paint ball guns. Later that evening, CW-1 unexpectedly encountered Mohamad Shnewer at a local store and was, therefore, unable to consensually record their conversation. CW-1 reported to law enforcement officers that Shnewer asked whether CW-1 had heard from CW-1's source for firearms and other weapons. CW-1 said that the source had just returned from Egypt. CW-1 observed that Shnewer appeared happy to learn that the source had recently returned from Egypt.

On or about February 26, 2007, Dritan Duka invited CW-1 to participate in a paint ball training exercise with Dritan Duka, Eljvir Duka, and their younger brother. CW-1 consensually recorded this exercise. Shortly before the training, CW-1 met with Dritan Duka and Eljvir Duka at Eljvir and Shain Duka's residence to prepare for the training. CW-1 and Eljvir Duka discussed CW-1's source for weapons, including AK-47 machine guns. Eljvir Duka asked CW-1 if CW-1's source could be trusted. Eljvir Duka explained that "...I had one brother buy [a gun] for me with a Pennsylvania license. It's my gun but he bought it under his name." Eljvir Duka then relayed to CW-1 the fact that Dritan Duka had previously attempted to purchase an AK-47 machine gun from an individual in Camden, New Jersey. Dritan Duka did not ultimately buy the weapon because he believed that he was being set up by the FBI. Dritan Duka then joined the conversation and stated, "I'm telling you, I almost bought a AK- 47 from an agent." Eljvir Duka then said, "Me right now we have the shotgun, we have the one which you was talking about, and we have the handgun .357 revolver." Eljvir Duka also expressed his knowledge that AK-47 machine guns are illegal: "You can't buy fully automatic... illegal." When CW-1 said to let CW-1 know if they wanted any weapons, Eljvir Duka responded: "Right now, ah, we want automatic hand guns and ah, my cousin wants one. Handgun." Later during the consensually recorded meeting, Eljvir Duka brought up the topic of CW-1's source for firearms and said, "Don't tell him about the AK-47 first. The handgun yes."

The paint ball exercise on February 26, 2007 occurred in a wooded area near Eljvir Duka and Shain Duka's residence. While CW-1 recorded it, Dritan Duka remarked that paint ball is good training for an attack, "In military they use this in U.S. Army... It's how they train you." Shain Duka also agreed that playing paint ball is good tactical training.

On or about March 9, 2007, CW-2 consensually recorded a meeting with Dritan Duka, Shain Duka, Serdar Tatar, and others during which Dritan Duka, Shain Duka, and Serdar Tatar discussed preparing for their operation in a military fashion.

On or about March 10, 2007, CW-2 consensually recorded conversations during a meeting with Dritan Duka and Shain Duka. When CW-2 asked Dritan Duka and Shain Duka about Serdar Tatar, Shain Duka explained that TATAR wanted to join the U.S. Army so that he could kill U.S. soldiers from the "inside." When CW-2 asked about Tatar again, Dritan Duka remarked, "He had only one mind, how to kill American soldiers." Later during the consensually recorded conversation, Dritan Duka and Shain Duka said that instead of waging jihad overseas, they could do so in the United States. Shain Duka also stated, "Because as far as people we have enough, 7 people. And we are all crazy. That's what is needed . . . ." Later in the conversation, Dritan Duka also stated, "For people, 7 people are a lot. We can do a lot of things with 7 people . . . We can do a lot of damage with 7 people . . . you do big things with 7 people." Toward the end of the meeting, Shain Duka suggested that they could also join the Army and "do them, we can."

On or about March 15, 2007, Dritan Duka invited CW-1 to participate in paint ball training with Dritan Duka, Shain Duka, and the Duka's younger brother. CW-1 met Dritan Duka and Shain Duka at Eljvir Duka and Shain Duka's residence to prepare for the paint ball training. After the paint ball exercise, CW-1 traveled to Shain Duka's and Eljvir Duka's residence in Cherry Hill where Dritan Duka gave CW-1 a business card on the back of which Dritan Duka wrote, among other things, "A-K 47 Kalichnikov." CW-1 consensually recorded this meeting, which captured Dritan Duka's conversation with CW-1 about CW-1's source for firearms. During the consensually recorded meeting, Dritan Duka again confirmed that he owned a black gun and a shotgun but acknowledged the illegality of doing so because he didn't have a green card. Dritan Duka also said, "I tell you now I need AK47s. If you can get them, give me two . . . AK-47, Kalichnikov, Russian." Dritan Duka then cautioned CW-1, "AK-47. Just don't talk on the phone." The consensual recording also captured CW-1 asking Dritan Duka to write down the name of the firearm Dritan Duka wanted to buy from CW-1's source.

On or about March 16, 2007, CW-1 turned over to the FBI the business card on which Dritan Duka had written "A-K 47 Kalichnikov." Later that day, CW-1 consensually recorded a conversation with Mohamad Shnewer during which CW-1 and Shnewer discussed Dritan Duka's request to buy AK-47 Russian machine guns. Shnewer asked CW-1 to have his source bring another AK-47 for Shnewer to purchase in addition to the two guns that Dritan Duka would purchase and the one gun that CW-1 claimed he would purchase. Specifically, Shnewer said, "Let him bring four. I know these guns as I used it in my country and I shot with it."

Shnewer also confirmed his knowledge about the illegality of such weapons: "It is not, there is nothing legal about it." Shnewer went on to say, "[t]he beauty of this one when we buy it now, is that you can go train on it and you can leave it on the semiautomatic setting, one shot at a time." When CW-1 and Shnewer discussed where to keep the AK-47s, Shnewer said that he would keep them at his residence in the attic.

Also during the meeting on March 16, 2007, Mohamad Shnewer said that Dritan Duka and Eljvir Duka knew the reason why they were getting the firearms. When CW-1 asked Shnewer whether Shnewer had changed his mind about Fort Dix, Shnewer responded:

> *Quite honestly there is the Navy base...You know where the stadiums are in Philadelphia? There is the Navy base and every year they have the Army–Navy ball game and they come and stay one or two weeks... the Navy base will then be full of people . . . You see this is an opportunity and the beauty of this location specially if you have the proper weaponry, is that you can hit it from where, do you know? From New Jersey.*

Shnewer also said that "everyone that was in the Poconos less one or two of them" were part of the group that would attack the U.S. military.

On or about March 23, 2007, CW-1 consensually recorded a conversation during a meeting with Dritan Duka. CW-1 told Dritan Duka that CW-1's source would provide a list of weapons that the source was selling, which CW-1 would then provide to Dritan Duka. CW-1 further stated that the source did not want to meet the Dukas. Dritan Duka remarked that it was better that the Dukas not meet CW-1's source.

Also on or about March 23, 2007, CW-2 consensually recorded a conversation during a meeting with Dritan Duka, Eljvir Duka, Shain Duka, and others. Shain Duka, Eljvir Duka, and Dritan Duka discussed Fort Dix and the nearby air force base. They also told CW-2 that Serdar Tatar's father owned a restaurant near Fort Dix and made deliveries onto the base.

On or about March 26, 2007, CW-1 consensually recorded a telephone call with Dritan Duka during which CW-1 explained that CW-1's source could not give CW-1 the list of firearms that weekend.

On or about March 28, 2007, CW-1 consensually recorded a telephone call with Dritan Duka during which CW-1 explained that his source had given CW-1 a list of the firearms that his source had available for sale. Dritan Duka said that he would call later and instruct CW-1 where to meet. Later, Dritan Duka called CW-1 (a call that CW-1 was unable to consensually record), instructing CW-1 to meet at a convenience store on Route 38 near Cooper Landing Road in Cherry Hill. CW-1 consensually recorded the ensuing meeting with Dritan Duka during which CW-1 handed the list of weapons to Dritan Duka. Law enforcement officers retained a photocopy of the list before CW-1 gave it to Dritan Duka. The list identified the following weapons for sale: "AK-47, M-16, M-60 machine gun, RPG, rocket, handgun semiautomatic, Sig Sauer 9 mm, Smith Wesson 9 mm, Smith Wesson revolver." The list also contained prices for the weapons.

On or about March 30, 2007, CW-1 consensually recorded a meeting with Mohamad Shnewer during which Shnewer asked, "[d]id you speak to the guy from Baltimore?" CW-1 explained that when Dritan Duka decided how many weapons they would need, CW-1 would instruct the source to come with the weapons. Shnewer said that $500—the price listed for the AK-47—was a "very good" price.

On or about April 5, 2007, CW-1 consensually recorded a telephone call with Mohamad Shnewer during which Shnewer asked CW-1 about the delivery of the weapons. CW-1 explained to Shnewer that Dritan Duka had to first provide CW-1 with the type and number of weapons Dritan Duka wanted to buy.

On or about April 6, 2007, CW-1 consensually recorded a meeting with Dritan Duka, among others. Dritan Duka stated to CW-1, "The list. I need all the, the AKs. The M16s and all the handguns." Dritan Duka then sought reassurance that CW-1's source could be trusted by asking CW-1 whether the source was religious and whether "there something they need to know." CW-1 asked, "Like what?" Dritan Duka responded, "To that list there was some stuff on the list that was heavy shit... the RPG." Dritan Duka then said,

> All of them [meaning the AK-47s] I need. He has four now... He has four AKs for five hundred dollars each...Each one. I want all of the AKs, all the M-16s, I think there was 4, no 5 AKs I think and... 4 M-16s. And I need all the handguns, one of each... Everything he had... Everything he had on the list... No everything he has except [the RPG and M-60 machine gun]."

During the meeting on April 6, 2007, Dritan Duka also expressed the need for secrecy:

> I just want to be safe brother, cause you understand? ... Cause I can afford, I . . . I just need to, cause I trust you brother, you understand? I got five kids so I don't wanna go down. People catch me like they think I'm a terrorist.

CW-1 and Dritan Duka also discussed how the sale of the weapons would take place. CW-1 said that the source would bring the weapons to New Jersey. In response, Dritan Duka said, "It's better, it's better if I get it over here [meaning New Jersey] cause we got no licenses."

On or about April 7, 2007, CW-2 consensually recorded a meeting with Eljvir Duka, Dritan Duka, and Shain Duka at Dritan Duka's residence. At one point, Eljvir Duka and Dritan Duka went upstairs to use a computer. After a period of time, Eljvir Duka and Dritan Duka came back downstairs and discussed a high-powered firearm they were reviewing on the computer and how a round fired from the weapon could penetrate a soldier's helmet.

On or about April 13, 2007, CW-1 consensually recorded a meeting with Dritan Duka and Mohamad Shnewer in which CW-1 responded that the source would bring the weapons in a couple of weeks. CW-1 told Dritan Duka and Mohamed Shnewer that they needed to have money, to which Dritan Duka responded that he had the money right now. CW-1 promised to call Dritan Duka when the source was ready to bring the weapons to New Jersey. CW-1 also told Shnewer about the weapons Dritan Duka had ordered. Shnewer discussed the RPG and the AK-47s, specifically referencing "Kalichnikov."

On or about April 27, 2007, CW-1 consensually recorded a meeting with Dritan Duka, during which Dritan Duka and CW-1 discussed the purchase of the weapons from CW-1;s source. CW-1 also consensually recorded a meeting with Mohamad Shnewer during which Shnewer told CW-1 that he only wanted to purchase the AK-47 machine gun at this time and to hold off on the sale of the RPG.

Surveillance Activities Defined

In the end, it was clear that these individuals were intent on an attack on a U.S. military installation. Understand that their *attack objectives* were the power grid, barracks, and soldiers. Their *surveillance objectives* were the front gate, internal security posts, perimeter vulnerabilities, and force protection measures.

Fortunately, one citizen made the right call to set the wheels in motion for law enforcement to intervene. Unfortunately, most, if not all, of their preoperations arguably would have gone undetected and a successful attack to an unknown degree would have occurred.

3.2.2.2 Homegrown Violent Extremist
Washington, DC, Metro

This plot differs from the others in that it was an FBI sting, in which a single individual, Farooque Ahmed, believing he was working with al-Qa'ida operatives, carried out reconnaissance on the Washington, DC, Metro (Figure 3.43). It is not clear in his indictment who first suggested the Metro as a target.

Ahmed, a naturalized U.S. citizen from Pakistan, had become increasingly radicalized by developments in the Middle East and southwest Asia and wanted to join al-Qa'ida's global jihad (Figure 3.44). He wanted to fight and kill Americans in Afghanistan, and while asking around to see how he could join a terrorist group, he met

Figure 3.43 Bomb plot.

Figure 3.44 Farooque Ahmed, a Pakistani American from Ashburn, Virginia.

individuals he believed to be affiliated with al-Qa'ida, but who, in fact, were FBI undercover agents, and he agreed to participate in a terrorist attack in the United States.

Ahmed was assigned to conduct surveillance and photograph Metrorail stations around

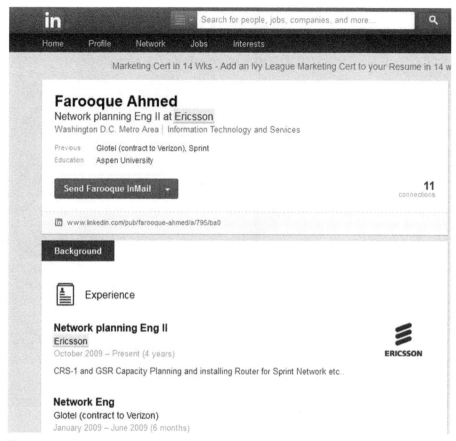

Figure 3.45 Farooque Ahmed's LinkedIn page showed him employed as a network engineer.

Washington, DC, which were to be the targets (Figure 3.45). Over a period of 6 months, Ahmed conducted reconnaissance of the stations, monitored security at a nearby hotel with a video and sketches, and made operational suggestions regarding the concealment of the explosive devices by utilizing rolling suitcases versus the traditional backpacks. The Metro is often utilized by air travels in route to Reagan International Airport and it is commonplace to see travelers aboard with large suitcases (Figure 3.46). FBI agents arrested him on

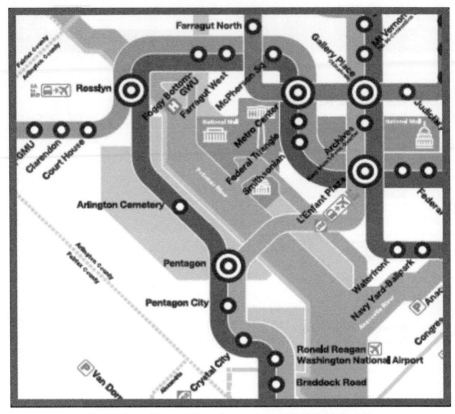

Figure 3.46 Metrorail stations around Washington, DC.

October 27, 2010, charging him with providing material support to a foreign terrorist organization and planning multiple bombings to cause mass casualties. He pleaded guilty and was sentenced to 23 years in prison.

Ahmed had been influenced by radical American cleric Anwar al-Awlaki, who had preached in northern Virginia until he fled to Yemen. Awlaki urged Muslims in the United States to carry out terrorist attacks, and Ahmed listened to his sermons online. Ahmed planned to carry out a rush-hour attack because it would cause the most casualties, clearly indicating that his objective was a high body count. Ahmed scouted several Metrorail targets, including the Arlington Cemetery, Courthouse, Crystal City, and Pentagon City stations. The Arlington Cemetery Station is on the Metro's Blue Line—one stop north of the Pentagon City station. The Crystal City and Pentagon City stations are on the Blue Line—one and two stops from the Pentagon City station. The Courthouse station is in Arlington, Virginia—on the Orange Line just before it connects to the Blue Line. All of these stations are used heavily by military personnel commuting to and from the Pentagon, and Ahmed's expressed desire was to "kill as many military personnel as possible." Of interest is Ahmed's purposeful avoidance of the Pentagon City station itself by selecting the two stations above and two below the Pentagon. This is directly contributable to the "hard target" the Pentagon presents, as well as known or perceived countersurveillance teams in and around the immediate area. Although he told undercover agents he was willing to be a martyr, Ahmed planned to carry out multiple bombings. He had no terrorist training but prepared himself for jihad by training in martial arts and the use of firearms.

Ahmed began to plan the operation in April 2010. He told undercover agents that he would be ready to begin his attacks in January 2011 after he completed a pilgrimage to Mecca in January. He said that an attack carried out during the afternoon rush hour, between 4:00 and 5:00 PM, would cause the most casualties. Ahmed recorded video images of the targeted stations. On the basis of this reconnaissance, he made suggestions about where the bombs should be placed to kill the most people in simultaneous attacks.

Security measures at Metro stations included CCTV, random patrols by Metro Transit Police Department officers, and a measure introduced in early 2010 called Blue TIDE (Terrorism Identification and Deterrence Effort), which teamed police officers with law enforcement officers from other agencies to conduct high-visibility, antiterrorism shows of force at Metro stations. Additionally, Visible Intermodal Prevention and Response teams of DHS–TSA's office of law enforcement worked these transportation areas with canine and behavioral detection officers working in concert. After Ahmed's arrest, the Washington Metro Area Transit Authority implemented random passenger screening and increased emphasis on enlisting passengers' assistance in identifying suspicious behavior.

Ahmed's quest to join violent jihad first came to the attention of the authorities in January 2010 as a result of a tip from a source inside the Muslim community. The FBI created the elaborate sting operation to assess Ahmed's intentions and capabilities.[9]

3.2.2.3 Antigovernment
Timothy McVeigh

Timothy McVeigh was an American militant who carried out the Oklahoma City bombing on April 19, 1995 (Figure 3.47). The explosion, which killed 168 people, was the deadliest

---

[9] *Carnage Interrupted: An Analysis of Fifteen Terrorist Plots Against Public Surface Transportation*, Brian Michael Jenkins and Joseph Trella.

Figure 3.47 Timothy McVeigh.

terrorist incident on U.S. soil until the September 11 attacks in 2001.

McVeigh was the middle child in a blue-collar family in rural New York State, and he expressed an interest in guns from an early age. He graduated from high school in June 1986 and spent a short period at a local business college. Around this time he first read *The Turner Diaries* (1978), an antigovernment, neo-Nazi tract written by William Pierce. The book, which details the truck bombing of the Washington, DC, headquarters of the Federal Bureau of Investigation, fueled McVeigh's paranoia about a government plot to repeal the Second Amendment of the U.S. Constitution, which guarantees the right "to keep and bear arms." He enlisted in the U.S. Army in 1988 and proved to be a model soldier, earning a Bronze Star for bravery in the Persian Gulf War

Figure 3.48 An army photograph with McVeigh in the back row (AP).

(1990−1991). He was a candidate for the Special Forces but dropped out of the program after only 2 days (Figure 3.48). The experience soured him on the military, and he took an early discharge and left the army in late 1991.

McVeigh returned to New York but was unable to find steady work. He reunited with Terry Nichols and Michael Fortier, friends from his days in the army, and sold guns at fairs throughout the United States. In March 1993 he drove to Waco, Texas, to observe the ongoing FBI siege of the Branch Davidian compound. He viewed the U.S. government's actions there as illegal, and it was during this time that McVeigh, Nichols, and Fortier made contact with members of militia groups in the Midwest.

In September 1994, McVeigh began plotting actively to destroy the Alfred P. Murrah Federal

Building in Oklahoma City. It is this author's understanding that McVeigh also conducted reconnaissance of the Minneapolis–St. Paul Federal Building, as well as others in various states, before deciding on Oklahoma City. Over the next 6 months, McVeigh and Nichols planned the bombing and acquired several tons (108 bags) of ammonium nitrate fertilizer, which, combined with fuel oil (three 55-gallon drums of drag-racing fuel), would provide the explosive power for the bomb. McVeigh and his co-conspirators used soup cans on a kitchen table to portray the truck bomb layout to include how to shape the charge for a maximum explosive effect into the target. While much of McVeigh's movements and activities prior to the attack are of suspect, it is with certainty he, and likely his coconspirator, was only able to establish the logistics of the attack through careful planning and surveillance of the target. McVeigh was a meticulous sort who left nothing to chance and reconnoitered the attack site on multiple occasions.

On April 19, 1995, the second anniversary of the deadly fire that ended the Branch Davidian siege, McVeigh parked the truck containing the bomb in front of the Alfred P. Murrah Building (Figure 3.49).

At 9:02 AM, the bomb went off, tearing off the front of the building, killing 168 people, and injuring more than 500. Slightly more than an hour later, McVeigh, driving a getaway car that he and Nichols had placed a few days earlier, was pulled over by an Oklahoma state police officer for a license plate violation. When the officer discovered that McVeigh was carrying a concealed handgun illegally, McVeigh was

Figure 3.49 The Ryder rental truck before the Oklahoma City bombing (AP).

arrested and held in jail, pending a trial on the gun charge. While he was in custody, McVeigh was identified as "John Doe No. 1," the primary suspect in the Oklahoma City bombing. Two days after the bombing, McVeigh was taken into federal custody, and Nichols turned himself in to authorities. The investigators found heaps of evidence implicating both McVeigh and Nichols in the bombing, such as bomb-making supplies, books on how to make a bomb, a hand-drawn map of Oklahoma City with the Alfred P. Murrah Building and the location of McVeigh's getaway car marked, and a copy of *Hunter*, a book written by the same author as *The Turner Diaries*, on Nichols' property.

The two were indicted in August 1995, and Attorney General Janet Reno stated that the government would seek the death penalty against both. McVeigh's month-long trial began in April 1997, and Fortier testified against him as part of a plea agreement. It took the jury 3 days to reach a unanimous guilty verdict. McVeigh was sentenced to death on June 13, 1997. Later that year, Terry Nichols was found guilty of conspiracy and eight counts of involuntary manslaughter and was sentenced to life in prison. On June 11, 2001, McVeigh became the first federal prisoner to be executed since 1963.

3.2.2.4 Single Issue

Radical Environmentalist Movement

During the past decade, dramatic changes in the nature of the domestic terrorist threat have been witnessed. In the 1990s, right-wing extremism overtook left-wing terrorism as the most dangerous domestic terrorist threat to the United States. During the past several years, however, special-interest extremism, as characterized by the Animal Liberation Front (ALF), the Earth Liberation Front (ELF), and related extremists, has emerged as a serious domestic terrorist threat. Special-interest terrorism differs from traditional right-wing and left-wing terrorism in that extremist special-interest groups seek to resolve specific issues rather than affect widespread political change. Such extremists conduct acts of politically motivated violence to force segments of society, including the general public, to change attitudes about issues considered important to the extremists' causes. Generally, extremist groups engage in much activity that is protected by constitutional guarantees of free speech and assembly. Law enforcement only becomes involved when the volatile talk of these groups transgresses into unlawful action. The FBI estimates that the ALF/ELF and related groups have committed more than 1100 criminal acts in the United States since 1976, resulting in damages estimated conservatively at approximately $110 million.

The ALF, established in Great Britain in the mid-1970s, is a loosely organized extremist movement committed to ending the abuse and exploitation of animals. The American branch of the ALF began its operations in the late 1970s. Individuals become members of the ALF not by filing paperwork or paying dues, but simply by engaging in "direct action" against companies or individuals who, in their view, utilize animals for research or economic gain or do some manner of business with those companies or individuals. "Direct action" generally occurs in the form of criminal activity designed to cause economic loss or to destroy the victims' company operations or property. The extremists' efforts have broadened to include a multinational campaign of harassment, intimidation, and coercion against animal-testing companies and any companies or individuals doing business with those targeted companies. Huntingdon Life Sciences (HLS) is one such company. The "secondary" or "tertiary" targeting of companies that have business or financial relationships with the target company typically takes the form of fanatical harassment of employees and interference with normal business operations under the threat of escalating tactics or even violence. The harassment is designed to inflict increasing economic damage until the company is forced to cancel its contracts or business relationship with the original target. Internationally, the best example of this trend involves Great Britain's Stop Huntingdon Animal Cruelty (SHAC) organization, a more organized subgroup within the extremist animal rights movement. SHAC has targeted the animal-testing company HLS and any companies with which HLS conducts business. While the SHAC organization attempts to portray itself as an information service or even a media outlet, it is aligned closely with the ALF and its pattern of criminal activities—many of which are taken against companies and individuals selected as targets by SHAC and posted on the Internet website of SHAC.

Investigation of SHAC-related criminal activity has revealed a pattern of vandalism, arsons, animal releases, harassing telephone calls, threats, and attempts to disrupt the business activities of not only HLS, but of all companies doing business with HLS. Among others, these companies include Bank of America, Marsh USA, Deloitte and Touche, and HLS investors, such as Stephens, Inc., which terminated their business relationships completely with HLS as a result of SHAC activities. Examples of SHAC activities include publishing on its website as a regular feature "Targets of the Week" for followers to target with harassing telephone calls and e-mails in order to discourage that company or individual from doing business with HLS.

In recent years, the Animal Liberation Front and the Earth Liberation Front have become the most active criminal extremist elements in the United States (Figure 3.50). Despite the destructive aspects of ALF and ELF's operations, their stated operational philosophy discourages acts that harm "any animal, human and nonhuman." In general, the animal rights and environmental extremist movements have adhered to this mandate. Beginning in 2002, however, this operational philosophy has been

Exhibit #1

Figure 3.50 The Animal Liberation Front and the Earth Liberation Front.

overshadowed by an escalation in violent rhetoric and tactics, particularly within the animal rights movement. Individuals within the movement have discussed actively targeting food producers, biomedical researchers, and even law enforcement with physical harm. Even more disturbing, however, is the recent employment of improvised explosive devices against consumer product-testing companies, accompanied by threats of more, larger bombings and even potential assassinations of researchers, corporate officers, and employees.

Activists are believed to engage in significant intelligence gathering against potential targets, including the review of industry/trade publications and other open source information, photographic/video surveillance of potential targets, obtaining proprietary or confidential information about intended victim companies through theft or from sympathetic insiders, and posting details about potential targets on the Internet for other extremists to use as they see fit.

The animal rights extremist and ecoterrorism movements are unlike traditional criminal enterprises that are often structured and organized. They exhibit remarkable levels of security awareness when engaged in criminal activity and are typically very knowledgeable of law enforcement techniques and the limitations imposed on law enforcement.[10]

There is a popular video of an ELF/ALF member, Rodney Coronado, attempting to incite students with ELF and ALF rhetoric to commit direct action activism and then demonstrating to students at Washington, DC-based American University how to make an incendiary device to commit arson for approximately $2. Coronado

---

[10] Statement of John E. Lewis, Deputy Assistant Director, Counterterrorism Division, Federal Bureau of Investigation before the Senate Judiciary Committee on May 18, 2004.

Figure 3.51 Rodney Coronado, an ELF/ALF member.

thinks he and ALF/ELF terrorists will be heroes 100 years from now[11] (Figure 3.51).

While the radical environmental movement is on the decline, animal and environmental rights extremists continue to pose a threat to American public safety. Domestic terrorism attacks outnumber international ones seven to one in the United States (LaFree, Dugan, Fogg, and Scott, 2006), and animal and environmental rights extremists compose a dangerous segment of domestic extremist movements (Smith, 1994). To date, most terrorism research has focused on international terrorism (Lum, Kennedy, and Sherley, 2006), and research on domestic political extremists has focused mostly on far-right extremists (Blazak, 2001). For example,

[11] AnimalRights.net

Gruenewald, Freilich, and Chermak (2009) identified over 320 studies on far-right extremists in the fields of criminology, political science, sociology, and terrorism, while a review of the literature on animal and environmental rights extremists in these disciplines found less than 70 studies. The criminal activities of these extremists are thus a neglected research topic.[12]

---

[12] *An Overview of Bombing and Arson Attacks by Environmental and Animal Rights Extremists in the United States, 1995–2010.* National Consortium for the Study of Terrorism and Responses to Terrorism.

4

CONDUCTING SURVEILLANCE DETECTION

CHAPTER OUTLINE

Abstract: By now you should be familiar with the terrorist preattack and attack methodology and their tactics, techniques, and procedures (TTPS)—indicators of preattack operations—and are now ready to understand the *paradigm shift* in surveillance and threat detection: to go from a *reactive to a proactive* security posture. We discuss proactive measures and learn how to exploit the vulnerabilities in terrorist and criminal's TTPs and how to stop them during their preattack operations.

Keywords: assessment, elicitation, infrastructure, observation, risk, security, surroundings, vulnerability

4.1 The Basics—Exploiting the Terrorist Preattack and Attack Methodology

By now you should be familiar with the terrorist preattack and attack methodology and their tactics, techniques, and procedures (TTPs)—indicators of preattack operations—and are now ready to understand the *paradigm shift* in surveillance and threat detection: to go from a *reactive to a proactive* security posture. This chapter discusses proactive measures, how to exploit the vulnerabilities in the terrorist and criminal's TTPs, and how to stop them during their preattack operations.

Risk assessment

The first step in proactive measures is to perform a risk assessment that addresses the potential threats against our facility (threat assessment), the need to identify our vulnerabilities (vulnerability assessment), and the importance of our facility and the consequences of an attack (criticality assessment).

- **Threat assessment.** We must look at our facilities from the perspective of the bad guys. We need to ask, who would want to attack our facility? What makes us a target for criminals and terrorists? If we handle large volumes of money, for example, then the threat would most likely be criminals. If we are a prominent government facility or are perceived as a symbol of authority, such as a federal center or the New York Exchange, then we can be considered as a target of political value by state-sponsored terrorists or sovereign citizens. If we are hosting a public event, what is the likelihood that we will be targeted by anarchists? Once we identify the threat, we must also assess their capabilities and urgency to strike. If an attack is executed, what would be its goal? To demolish the building? Inflict mass casualties? Cause economic distress?

- **Vulnerability assessment**. We need to study our facility to determine its weaknesses. What are the likely targets? People? A particular building? The destruction of equipment? How possible would it be to initiate an attack on those targets? What are the security measures? Where are the breach points? Considering the threat, are we a "hard" target or a "soft" target? Would your facility be classified as a high-value target? The key to a vulnerability assessment is to think like the bad guys.

- **Criticality assessment**. What are the consequences of an attack on your facility? How critical are the components of your facility? For example, an attack on the electrical grid into your building could affect your ability to evacuate, contain fire, and mitigate further damage. If a nearby bridge was destroyed, how would that affect the ability of first responders to reach your facility?

4.1.1 Observation Skills

The first step of our proactive measures is to know what you're looking for. But what are you looking for? What are you watching?

No doubt you will be looking for suspicious behavior—for what is "normal vs not normal." For example, you see a group of young men carrying heavily laden backpacks arrive together at a train station. They then split up and go separate ways or board different cars of the same train. What does this mean? Was this suspicious behavior?

To understand if this was "normal or not normal," we have to put this behavior in the context that we know terrorists and criminals have specific *surveillance objectives*. They will identify facility vulnerabilities and surveillance targets. They will then use intelligence gathered from surveillance to select attack objectives. As part of our vulnerability assessment, we have identified our vulnerabilities—both the likely targets within our facility and possible gaps in our security that would allow the bad guys to reach those targets.

We have to determine how the terrorists conduct surveillance to gather intelligence about our vulnerabilities. Our vulnerability assessment should have identified terrorists' attack objectives—their targets. The question is where can the terrorists place themselves to remain inconspicuous and collect the information they need to plan and execute an attack? If we've identified the front entrance as a vulnerability, where would the bad guys need to loiter to maintain a direct line of sight? Likewise, if a parking garage or a power substation is chosen as a target objective, where would the terrorists have to position themselves to surveil those facilities? Is our building facing a public sidewalk? Are there hotels or offices that overlook our facility? Do these locations offer the opportunity for surveillance?

Security officers must look at a facility and determine what would be the terrorists' attack objectives. If the facility was attacked, for what purpose? A bank, obviously, would be attacked to steal money, but what about a train station? The objective would probably be to inflict mass casualties. How would terrorists conduct such an attack? In this case, we need to ask ourselves: what measures do we have available to prevent an attack? Is there a significant guard presence? What sort of monitoring do we have in place? How often do we sweep for unattended packages and backpacks? If an attack on our facility is to gain maximum media attention for propaganda, such as the planned attacks against Fort Dix, then we can assume that the attack objective is twofold: first penetrate our security perimeter and then execute the attack.

- Identify locations from which long-term surveillance can be performed, what we call hostile surveillance locations (HSLs)—*red zones.*

Terrorists select surveillance zones to optimize their observation of your facility, a place where they can "perch" and maintain a line of sight to gather information to support their preattack planning. We designate such a zone as a HSL—a *red zone.* Identifying red zones will allow you to focus your time and limited resources to specific areas. Perches are usually in an elevated position because people seldom look up. An elevated position can also provide for a more comprehensive view of your facility. When you conduct countersurveillance, look at roofs, balconies, overpasses, and bridges. Surveillants also search for cover—places where they can linger and observe inconspicuously: a bus stop, a park, or a coffee shop.

- Identify and describe electronic security measures. Are there any video cameras? Alarms? Where are they? What type? What area do they cover?

For proactive measures, we need to assess whether our electronic measures are situated too close to our perimeter. If we compare our facility to the model of concentric rings of security, we will most likely see that almost all electronic security is placed to protect the inner ring—our immediate perimeter. Unfortunately, by the time a terrorist arrives at this point, an attack is either imminent or under way. In too many cases, surveillance cameras capture images of the terrorist blowing himself up when our goal is to identify the terrorist beforehand and deter the attack. Consequently, we need to expand our electronic surveillance farther outward. Instead of aiming all your video cameras along the perimeter, dedicate some to monitor designated red zones. Additionally, electronic surveillance must be augmented with human countersurveillance to determine patterns of suspicious behavior. Suppose we notice a group of people passing by our front entrance and, an hour later, the same group passes by again. Then next week, we observe the same group passing by one more time. *Suspicious?* You bet. Detecting the group isn't sufficient, what we must do is remain vigilant to detect patterns of suspicious behavior. *Normal* vs *not normal.*

- Document security procedures through note taking and surreptitious photography or video. What is the access protocol for your facility? Do you have to show a badge? Swipe the badge to unlock a door or use a punch code? Are vehicles searched? How do you transport classified material—in special pouches or couriers? How often do you empty your trash? How do you get rid of shredded material?

For proactive measures, security officers must understand what they observe about our vulnerabilities and how to report them. Always be asking how can the bad guys bypass our security procedures? What can we do to make our facility a "hard target" and encourage the terrorists to move to another facility, a "softer target."

- Study the security force. How many guards? What is their gender and ethnicity? Where are they located? What is their dress? Do they wear a uniform? What kind of weapons? Do they have dogs? Are the guards competent? Can they be distracted?

We can address these concerns through training and the adoption of random antiterrorism measures (RAMs). Security supervisors must assure that their security force is trained adequately to recognize and mitigate the facility's vulnerabilities. Concurrently, RAMs keeps the bad guys guessing about your security measures. For example, if you search every third person entering your facility, on the next day change the pattern to search every fifth. On random occasions, have a show of force present such as marked police cars parked outside your entrance. This makes the bad guys wonder about your security posture. On public transportation venues, you should deploy search dogs and armed police officers or guards randomly.

Use officers trained in behavioral detection to watch the reaction among the public and recognize suspicious behavior. You may catch the guy approaching a turnstile, who then notices the search dogs and suddenly turns to leave. No matter how well-equipped and trained your security force may be, however, remember that complacency and predictability are your constant enemies against effective surveillance detection.

- How does your facility react with first responders such as an ambulance? How long does it take for first responders to arrive after being notified? What are the approach routes? (The police, fire engines, and ambulances may arrive from different directions.) Where do they enter the facility? What kind of vehicles and equipment do they use? What measures are in place to verify their identity, such as special badges or code words? For example, would it be possible for terrorists to commandeer an ambulance to gain access into your facility?

An effective security program should create a relationship with your first responders. All partners—your security force, police, fire fighters, and ambulances—should articulate their concerns and agree to procedures to assure an effective response that does not compromise your facility's security. Perform drills to familiarize everyone with the protocols and to work the kinks out of the process. Furthermore, as part of your vulnerability assessment, consider that an attack on your facility may be a ploy to summon the first responders, *who could be the actual target of an attack*! Since we expect first responders to use the shortest and quickest route to your facility (something the terrorists would have noted), you should monitor the approach routes adjacent to your facility and have contingency plans in place.

Basic training for us: Honing our skills as security specialists

We must understand surveillance.

- What are the terrorists' objectives? What is the difference between surveillance and attack objectives?
  - Surveillance objectives are those locations from which the terrorist seeks to gather intelligence for their preattack planning.
  - Attack objectives are those targets the terrorist seeks to damage or destroy.
- What are the terrorists' TTPs? What behavior will they exhibit to surveil you and not get caught?
- What are the terrorists' methodologies? What are they doing and why? How are they changing TTPs to hide their surveillance?

The basis for proactive measures is that we must improve *observational awareness* by learning what to look for.

- What is the baseline activity around your facility? What is the "pattern of life?" When do people arrive for work? How do they arrive at work—cars, busses, or light rail? Where do employees park? What entrances do they use? Do they form long queues? When are deliveries made? Who accepts these deliveries?

When do visitors arrive? Where do they enter? Where do taxis wait for fares? Where are the bus stops?

- Consider your surrounding environments. What is "normal?" Someone waiting at a nearby bus stop is *normal,* but someone letting several busses go by and not boarding one is definitely *not normal.*
- Pay careful attention to surveillance zones, especially those identified as HSLs—*red zones.*

Observational awareness can be improved by using a four-step observation process

1. Use a systematic method to avoid missing suspicious behavior that may blend in with your surroundings. Develop a grid to pinpoint activities in nearby buildings. Where are the "perches" (Figure 4.1)?
2. Understanding the context of activities in your surroundings:
- People. What are the typical behaviors of people around your facility? How are they dressed? How do they interact?
- Identify and avoid visual distracters. What looks "not normal?" and why? Could it be misdirection to hide other suspicious activity? Suppose a pretty woman decides to practice yoga at the park across the street from your facility. Your security officers focus their attention on her and miss the surveillant who is documenting the coverage of your closed-circuit televisions(CCTVs).
- Train yourself to avoid tunnel vision. Don't fixate on one person or activity and miss something else. Understand what is "normal." What is the pattern? Suppose a car stalls

Figure 4.1 A grid used to show possible "perches" in nearby buildings.

outside your facility and blocks the entrance, causing gridlock at morning rush hour. While your security officers help clear the entrance, a surveillant may use that stalled car as a distraction and try to enter your facility on foot.

- You can determine what is "*not* normal," that is, suspicious behavior.
  - Clue in on the "What the ?????"—of something definitely out of the "normal," for example, a man loitering and waving a picnic basket in the direction of your building. Who carries a picnic basket? And, what's in the basket? What about "bad" behavior or demeanor? Two men start to fight or threaten employees. Could that incident be a distraction?

- Why would someone take a picture of ????? Wouldn't it be suspicious for someone to be taking photos of your gates or of the power lines servicing your building?
- Rapid cognition—your "gut feeling." Your intuition may be piecing together clues that your consciousness has not yet recognized. You may be picking up on the surveillant's nervousness or that he is performing activities that are "not normal."

3. Remembering.

- Create a "snapshot" into your long-term memory. Decide that what you are seeing is "not normal" and remember as much as possible.
- Practice *visual tagging*. Select noteworthy details so you can describe the person(s). Note body size and type, specific colors of clothing, mannerism, or equipment carried. Was the person short and dark and wearing a gray jacket? Did he use a special camera? Was he observing your facility with binoculars?
- Use *visual chunking*. Gather smaller details in larger groups of information. Perhaps a suspicious person was tall and heavyset with a very hairy head. You may refer to him as "Sasquatch" as a way to chunk his appearance visually.

4.1.2 Surveillance Detection Activities

What is surveillance? Here is a rather usable definition provided by terrorists (al-Qa'ida surveillance training manual recovered in Herat, Afghanistan, 2001):

> It is putting persons, things, or places under fixed and steady surveillance for a continuous or limited period of time or surveillance of mobile targets as they move

from place to place in an attempt to get to these targets gathering intelligence information about the enemy.

A dedicated team of trained surveillance operations specialists working inside the red zones to identify suspicious activity and maintaining real-time capability to identify those bad actors is arguably the number one preventive measure a high-value target or critical infrastructure could take.

Additionally, the multitude of security and routine personnel in and around a facility should be trained on what suspicious activity looks like, or surveillance recognition. These eyes and ears are force multipliers that feed your intelligence collection around your facility.

4.1.2.1 Surveillance Recognition

What do terrorists observe during surveillance?

- They are concerned primarily with their potential targets' vulnerabilities. How easy is it for the bad guys to get at us?
- Where are our weapons? Do we have fixed gun emplacements? Are the guard buildings reinforced? Armored cars? What type of weapons" Pistols? Rifles? Machine guns? Mines? Nonlethal weapons (tear gas, Tasers, rubber bullets)?
- What are our standard operating procedures? How do employees enter our facility? How are deliveries made? What happens during an evacuation drill?
- What are the physical attributes of our facility? Where are the buildings located? How close are they to the traffic grid? Are there fences? Windows?

- What is your routine "pattern of life?" When do employees arrive for work? When is quitting time? When do the guards change shifts?

Shift changes are a favored time for surveillance by the bad guys. During shift changes, those security officers on duty become preoccupied with the end of their shift and lower their vigilance. Terrorists will observe and document the habits of the security officers to determine the "pattern of life." What is the schedule for shift changes? What is the protocol of the shift change? Is there a formal exchange of information, a debriefing, or is it a casual assumption of duties—outgoing guards high-fiving the incoming shift?

- What are the ingress/egress routes into your facility? Are there checkpoints? Where is the parking lot? Public transportation?
- Special mission coverage. The terrorists may seek certain vulnerabilities depending on the goals of the attack. For example, they may want to learn how your electrical power supply works in order to disable your security systems.

Terrorists may expand their surveillance from facilities to individuals and will key on the following specifics about you (especially when traveling abroad).

- Your dress, shoes, and jewelry. What kind of clothes do you typically wear? Shoes are important details because people seldom think that others notice what is worn on their feet. Foreigners often wear shoes of a type not available locally. Plus, when people change disguises, they often forget to switch shoes.

Additionally, people fail to remove or change jewelry.

- Your speech. If you're in a foreign country, the locals will obviously speak a different language, and your English will sound different from theirs.
- Flash U.S. currency—good old Yankee dollars—and everyone will assume you are an American.
- Behavior. Everyone acts a little different in a new environment. Try not to stand out.
- Products. We Americans love our gizmos and toys. Take a look around and see if anyone one else is wearing earbuds. Using an iPad? An e-reader? Carrying a laptop?
- Tattoos. Not only are tattoos a unique and permanent identifier, in many countries, their use may be frowned upon, so your tattoos will peg you as "one of them."
- Do what you can to avoid standing out:
  - Stay away from collection areas—those places that mark you as a foreigner, for example, the closest fast-food joint that you recognize from home or a newsstand with English-language magazines.
  - Avoid pairing up. It's comforting to find another American so far from home, but between the two of you, you've just doubled your signature.
  - Even the smallest details could betray you. Soldiers and ex-military tend to march even when walking casually, often in step and beginning each walk with their left foot. "Forward march!"
  - Your use of a cell phone could mark you as different, as behavior "not normal" in that environment.
  - The same goes for e-mail and texting.

- Have some kind of practical cover for your status. Act like a visiting scholar or a tourist.

We just reviewed what the bad guys are looking for about you. Now what about when you are looking for them? Be aware of the following.

- Foot surveillance, of two to three individuals working together. One might be the lookout for the other who is using a camera.
- Mobile surveillance from bicycles, scooters, cars, motorcycles, busses, sport-utility vehicles, or trucks. A moving vehicle is a great platform for making videos.
- Prolonged static surveillance using an operative who blends into the normal pattern of life. It could be someone disguised as a beggar, shoe shiner, fruit or food vendor, street sweeper, or a newspaper or flower seller. A homeless person makes for a great disguise as he is practically invisible and hangs around all day doing nothing but watching.
- The discreet use of still cameras and/or video recorders. Someone taking surreptitious photos wants to hide their behavior—definitely "not normal."
- Taking notes. Is it "normal" for someone to be taking notes of your activities?
- What about multiple sets of clothing, identifications, sketching materials (paper, pencils), still/video cameras, or binoculars?
- Unusual or prolonged interest in security measures or personnel, entry points, shift changes, and access controls.
- Individuals noticeably observing security reaction drills or procedures.

- Persons exhibiting unusual behavior such as the nervous shifting of weight, drumming fingers, sighing or exhaling dramatically, staring, or looking away quickly when eye contact is made.

4.1.2.2 Elicitation Recognition

What is elicitation? Elicitation means to draw out something that is latent or hidden. It is a way to collect information—in surveillance, it is the art of extracting information through the manipulation of routine conversation.

Why is elicitation so effective? Because it

- Takes advantage of cultural weakness and proclivities to be friendly and answer questions.
- Usually occurs in a relaxed atmosphere when the subject is open to casual conversation—at a bar, in a coffee shop, or waiting in line.
- The subject is often unaware and does not recall what information was disclosed. During the course of a conversation, you could reveal where you work, where you live, what kind of a car you drive, where you were born, or if you have children and not realize you had done so.

During an elicitation, wheels are then set in motion to

- Capitalize on the American tendency to answer questions from a stranger/friend/professional. If someone needs help or is curious about us, we feel flattered by the attention and like to respond in kind.
- Identify exploitable traits (e.g., financial problems, disgruntled worker, disagree with formal policy). The person asking questions will try to

establish rapport with you, to find some common ground that will get you to open up. You will be engaged in conversation that prompts you to vent and drop your guard. Who doesn't like to complain about work? Who wouldn't like to make more money? Sports are a great conversation starter.

- Establish friendship with the target (you). Once a bond has been created, you feel free to talk often and discuss more topics.

We can sometimes be our own worst enemy!

Elicitation is a nonthreatening, highly effective, and easy-to-disguise intelligence-gathering technique. This is how it's done: The person will use *stacking techniques* to guide the conversation from macro topics (broad subjects) to micro topics (specific details).

The person asking questions will start with *macro topics*:

- Beautiful weather.
- Can gas prices get any more outrageous?
- How about them Giants?

These will be general questions to get you talking and drop your guard.

Next the conversation will funnel to *micro topics*, For example, if you answered enthusiastically about the Giants, then you might get a general comment about New York. "The humidity there is unbelievable."

Note that you weren't asked a question directly, but the statement was made to elicit a response. The person conducting the elicitation has specific information he or she wants from you and will steer the conversation to get that information. The person will pay close attention to your replies and observe how you respond.

The person could use the following.

- *A false statement that provokes a response from you.* Such a statement might be "Only people with connections can get anything done around here." And you would feel obliged to correct them.
- *Flattery.* Who doesn't like to be complimented or noticed? "You must be very important." "That's a sharp coat," which leads to you to think, *this person likes me. I like him, too. Let me tell you a little more about myself.*
- *Complaining.* "Rush-hour traffic is terrible." Who doesn't like to commiserate?
- *Mutual interest.* "Who do you think will make the hockey playoffs?"
- *Direct questions.* "What do you do?"

After gathering the information, the conversation will be steered back to macro topics. That way, the last thing you remember from the exchange are general responses about benign subjects. In this scenario, the conversation can start with sports, then mention nearby traffic, discuss how people arrive at work, what you do, and finish with a discussion about the best places to eat in the area.

Does elicitation really work? *Absolutely.*

During an exercise conducted by a government counterintelligence training academy, students were sent into a local shopping mall with instructions to approach strangers and elicit:

1. High school attended.
2. Home address.
3. Mortgage amount.
4. Place of employment.
5. Cell phone number.
6. Banking establishment.
7. Name and date of birth of spouse and children.
8. First romantic experience.

Incredibly, all the information from the collection list was usually obtained within *19 minutes*.

Terrorists will select targets who can be especially vulnerable to elicitation, such as disgruntled employees or those with personal problems such as drug or alcohol abuse.

Being aware of elicitation techniques will alert you of what is "not normal" and that the person initiating the conversation may be a terrorist or a criminal conducting preattack operations.

It is important for law enforcement officials to remember that while a small innocuous piece of information may seem harmless in and of itself, these bits of so-called "harmless" information gathered over time by terrorists could allow them to piece together information that would be considered "sensitive knowledge." This is often referred to as the "grain of sand" technique of intelligence gathering. These types of activities are analogous to the street criminal "casing a joint" and warrant at least a field interview, the same as any other suspicious activity.

In addition to unofficial inquiry, some terrorist organizations have been known to go to the extent of infiltrating government contracting agencies in both information-sensitive roles and noninformation-sensitive roles (e.g., janitors, mail room workers), thereby allowing their own personnel to be in key positions to elicit information on potential targets more easily (Razzaq, 2003; SCN, 2005).

4.1.3 Recording and Reporting Skills

As security officers, our two most important proactive measures to stopping the bad guys are *identifying* and *documenting* suspicious activity. Thus far, we've reviewed terrorist and criminals' TTPs and learned how to *identify* suspicious behavior. We've realized the need for a risk assessment to identify the threat, determine our vulnerabilities, and examine the criticality of our facility. Now we must take the next step and *document* suspicious behavior through the use of effective recording and reporting skills. The point of recording and reporting is that this information will be forwarded "upstream" to other operations or agencies whose analysts will study that suspicious activity, connect the dots, and advance the process from *surveillance detection* to *threat detection*.

Recording. Earlier we discussed techniques of observation such a visual tagging to help us remember key details about a subject. We need to document those details in writing or using photography or video. Every security officer should carry a pen or pencil and a notebook. In those cases where it might be impractical to write notes, the officer may choose to use a camera or an audio recorder. Smartphones may have apps that help document information.

Reporting. Every security operation should have a suspicious activity reporting (SAR) process that includes a protocol for reporting suspicious behavior. Security officers must know who to report that behavior to; in turn, the security operation should know how to and to whom those reports are forwarded to. Don't wait until the end of your shift to write the report. Write it as soon as possible while the details remain fresh. Your SAR process should include forms or a method that facilitates the documentation of information with prompts to ensure that all necessary details are included. All security officers must know that their reports should provide the following.

- **Paint a picture.** The report should provide context to the suspicious behavior. What about that behavior was "not normal?" What were the circumstances—the pattern of life—that made you perceive the behavior as suspicious activity?
- **Be fully descriptive.** The report should provide sufficient details. What was the nature of the subject's suspicious behavior? What did the subject look like and what was he wearing? Did the subject exhibit nervous tics? Where was he? Was he alone? What was the weather like? If in a vehicle, what kind? What was the license number? Color, make,

and model? Did the subject take photos? With what, a camera or a cell phone?

- **Tell a story.** What about the subject first caught your attention? What was the subject doing? How did the subject proceed through your field of view? What path did he take? How long was the subject present and when did he leave? Where did the subject go? How, on foot or on a vehicle?

- **Be legally defensible.** The report may be regarded as evidence in a court of law. The security officer must articulate what behavior by the subject was determined to be suspicious and what prompted the officer to take appropriate follow-up actions.

As an example, at first you might write a SAR that reads as follows: On Tuesday afternoon I observed a man dressed in a red shirt and blue jeans stop at the corner adjacent to the facility main entrance and take several pictures.

The basics are there, but much more detail is needed to help analysts understand the situation. You must train yourself to record a more comprehensive report of what was observed and list specific details, such as what follows. On Tuesday, at 2:15 PM, I observed a man hustle across the busy street that fronts our main entrance. The man was about 5 foot 9, slender, had a ruddy complexion, and dark hair that reached his collar. He wore plastic sunglasses, a long-sleeved red shirt, new blue jeans, and white athletic shoes. The man walked across the street and stopped beside the lamppost at the corner adjacent to the main entrance. He bent over as if to tie one shoe, but in his hand he held a smartphone that he pointed at the entrance and at the security cameras as if taking photographs. Afterward, he stood and walked along the sidewalk and then crossed the street again to disappear around the corner. The weather was clear and the temperature in the 80s.

A standardized report format will both encourage the comprehensive enumeration of details and make it easier to retrieve that information at a later date. For example, the report should ask for the time and weather conditions of the suspicious activity. This may help analysts determine a pattern of suspicious behavior of a possible threat. Rather than invent the wheel, the security supervisor should explore commercial products such as TrapWire to record, store, and share suspicious activities. At the same time, don't be lulled into the routine reiteration of information onto a form—be prepared to address situations that fall outside the documentation format.

Additionally, your SAR process should build and maintain institutional memory. You can expect security officers to cycle through your facility, and they all should have the means to become familiar with your surveillance detection history. Furthermore, accurate and thorough documentation will enable even a new chief of security operations to maintain a vigilant and effective security posture.

4.1.4 Hostile Surveillance Locations

We've discussed that terrorists and criminals will establish surveillance objectives as part of their preattack planning. To assure a successful attack, the bad guys will need to collect as much intelligence as possible about your vulnerabilities. From the risk assessment that you conduct on your facility, you should identify your vulnerabilities (through the vulnerability assessment), which are the possible targets and the breach points in your security. Once our vulnerabilities are recognized, we must ask ourselves the following: how can the bad guys get the necessary intelligence to exploit our weaknesses and execute an attack? We know that terrorists and criminals will use a long-term surveillance study to collect information about your pattern of life. The specific areas the bad guys need to occupy to conduct that surveillance are called hostile surveillance locations, often referred to as *red zones*.

Knowing your red zones is key to your security proactive measures.

Identifying your HSLs presents a significant advantage to mitigate the risk to your facility, as it allows you to detect suspicious behavior by terrorists and criminals. In other words, *the bad guys will self-identify themselves* because they must move into a hostile surveillance location to collect the information they need to plan and execute an attack.

Hostile surveillance locations have specific criteria. They must be in a location that

- Provides for long-term surveillance of your facility's targets and breach points. Terrorists and criminals will observe and analyze your security measures and counterdetection efforts. What can your guards see? Where are your CCTVs?

- Allows the surveillant to study your pattern of life. What are the normal hours of operation? When is shift change? At what time are you most vulnerable?
- Facilitates the bad guys' ability to remain inconspicuous. They will attempt to blend in with your surroundings. They know the importance of safety in numbers and will attempt to hide among the random faces that come and go with the ebb and flow of the business day. They will also loiter in places where people are expected to wait, such as a bus stop or taxi stand.
- Allows them to "perch." Typically, a perch is located in an elevated position because people seldom look up. However, a perch can be any spot where a bad guy can loiter undetected.

As you identify potential red zones, ask yourself: What can the bad guys see from these HSLs? What kind of information can terrorists and criminals collect? How can they blend in?

Where are the areas around your facility that pedestrians tend to wait? Does your parking facility allow public access? If people wait in parking to pick up employees, where do they park? What can they see from that spot? What about loading zones? Taxi stands? For example, at a bus stop, at what time do people usually wait? What busses service the stop? How long do people usually wait? Who are those people? Employees from your facility? Other commuters? What is their typical behavior? Knowing this information, you could then recognize when someone was loitering at the bus stop for a suspicious length of time. Suppose a commuter lets several busses pass. Wouldn't you ask what is that person waiting for? *Normal* or *not normal?*

What if your facility sits close to a public park? When do people usually congregate there? What is their typical behavior? Look for "not normal" behavior. Would someone push a stroller and then park it facing your front entrance during a cold, icy day? Is anyone walking in a suspicious manner, that is, stiffly and exhibiting nervous tics? Are they secretly manipulating a device that could be a hidden camera?

Look up. Are there perches—roof tops, high rises, bridges, or overpasses—where someone could watch you?

As you map locations that could be red zones, look for connections. For example, would you happen to notice that whenever VIPs arrive at your facility is someone watching with binoculars from the balcony of an adjacent building? Or the taxi that turns away fares? Look beyond your immediate perimeter. The bad guys will note your countersurveillance measures, such as line of sight by your guards and the location of your CCTVs. Where could a surveillant plant himself and not get noticed?

Consider coffee shops and diners close to your facility. Use this as an opportunity to expand your definition of a hostile surveillance location. Even if a coffee shop does not overlook your facility, what kind of critical information could a surveillant glean from its customers? How about who works at your facility? What do they wear? What kind of badges do they carry?

What do they gossip about? Would this shop provide the occasion for a terrorist or criminal to gather intelligence through elicitation? How could you spot suspicious behavior among the customers? Just as the bad guys study your pattern of life, you should study the pattern of life around you to ascertain what normal behavior is.

Your security officers should be familiar with all your red zones, both their locations and what places of your facility they can surveil. Your countersurveillance effort should include monitoring these hostile surveillance locations with either dedicated CCTVs or undercover security personnel.

Knowing that you will be targeted by terrorists and criminals, you might consider using red zones to draw the bad guys where you can better identify and countersurveil them. The logic being, who but a bad guy would loiter in that area?

Know your red zones and use them to your advantage!

4.1.5 Team Operations

4.1.5.1 Team Structures

There are several different types of team structures organizations can implement to manage their surveillance detection programs. These team structure methods include formal, mobile, and in-country training teams. All three methods can be used simultaneously or independently. Some organizations have designated surveillance detection teams, whereas others train and set up procedures for all employees to be able to detect and report suspicion activities. Setting up surveillance detection teams can be a costly and resource-intensive process. Some organizations have set up formal teams in high-threat countries where labor is not as costly, such as Indonesia, Pakistan, and Kuwait. However, basic elements of surveillance detection can be applied across all organizations regardless of their size.

Formal team. A formal team consists of a designated surveillance detection program with leadership and oversight, coordination, analysis, and dedicated surveillance detection personnel. A surveillance detection team may sometimes operate at an off-site location, minimizing a physical presence at the targeted facility. Procedures are established for the team to detect preoperation surveillance, record biographical information, report sightings, and set up methods to provide suspicious incident reporting to local authorities or private guards to interdict. Most formal teams have an off-site coordinator who inputs the information into a database to correlate the sightings. This person also coordinates reports with the individual who has complete oversight, such as the local security manager. Most organizations surveyed use the same vetting process that they would use for hiring of their local security personnel. Typically, organizations use formal surveillance teams in high-threat environments and at crucial infrastructure facilities.

Mobile. Some organizations also have mobile teams implemented, which can be deployed for short periods of time at a facility location.

A mobile structure can be very useful in deploying a team on very short notice. However, given their mobility, it may take several weeks to establish a base of operations. Organizations generally use a mobile structure to cultivate relationships with the local community in an effort to establish a formal method of reporting. Most organizations report that mobile teams are usually used at facilities where internal staff have reported a spike in sightings.

In-country training. The concept of a surveillance detection program should be used among all hired staff. Employees are the first line of defense and should know how to report suspicious behavior. Several organizations have mandatory surveillance detection and countersurveillance programs set up for employees and family members in high-threat regions. In addition, organizations have strategically set up formal methods to detect and report information with employees who have a routine presence outside of the facility, such as maintenance crews, local guards, drivers, and front lobby personnel.

4.2 Incorporation of Video Technology

The 18th-century utilitarian philosopher Jeremy Bentham envisioned the perfect environment for watching over convicts using persistent surveillance. The design was known as the "panopticon," and it allowed constant surveillance by prison guards unbeknownst to inmates. The panopticon design placed prisoners in cells around a central observation tower. From the tower, convicts could be watched, but could not see who was watching. The architectural design of using surveillance as a threat, Bentham believed, was enough to compel prisoners to behave to the point that actual observation would most likely be unnecessary. Bentham also believed that the concept of persistent surveillance would not only grant unrestrained power to observe whenever desired, but would lead indirectly to the power to control the actual behavior of those being watched.

The ideology behind panopticon was not fully appreciated during Bentham's time. Ironically, two centuries later a parallel ideology of persistent surveillance is eagerly being sought by military strategists. Information gained through the use of persistent surveillance is believed essential for U.S. forces against adversarial challenges faced in 21st-century warfare.[1]

The debate rages over video technology usage in our current society. In fact, to address the issue would and could (and has) take an entire book in and of itself.

This chapter only covers the purposes of utilization of CCTV in threat detection operations and stresses true integration of "eyes on the ground" working in conjunction with CCTV capabilities or "eyes in the tower."

For fixed site threat detection, this allows for multiple advantages. With ground forces calling

---

[1] *Defining Conditions for the Use of Persistent Surveillance*, Cristina Cameron Fekkes, Major, U.S. Air Force Naval Postgraduate School, 2009.

into a **dedicated** CCTV operator, the team can play zone defense for a mobile bad guy. This allows the threat detection ground team to remain static and prevent the tell-tail sign of following a subject. The subject is captured on CCTV for evidentiary reasons and the video is used for future (or past) identification. This setup requires excellent team work throughout the team, reliable covert communications, and senior-level buy in of a threat detection program.

Closed-circuit televisions can also be fixed on a facility's red zone in order to capture anomalies within its field of view. Currently, there are numerous artificial intelligence (AI) software programs. It is this author's opinion that BRS Labs "AISight" is best of breed and several years in front of the industry. Advanced behavior recognition in crowded, unstructured environments, facial recognition, body pose, gaze tracking, slow person tracking, fast person tracking, and signal-based surveillance tracking are rapidly coming to market.

There are scores of papers regarding AI in CCTV to identify and track a bad actor. Two papers of note for recommended reading are:

- *The Ontology and Processing of Human Bodies: Appearance, Posture, Motion, Behavior, Actions, and Interactions Applied to Sequences of 2-D and 3-D Digital Video Surveillance* DataDecember, 2009. Vice President W. Swonger, Advanced TechnologyCoherix, Inc.
- *Advanced Behavior Recognition in Crowded Environments.* Authors: Ming-Ching Chang,

Weina Ge, Nils Krahnstoever, Ting Yu, Ser Nam Lim, and Xiaoming Liu.

It is impertaive that security pratitioners utilize all of the various resources at their disposal in an effective, cohesive way. Video played a crucial role in identifiying the Boston Marathon attackers and highlights the use and manner for which security proffesionals must consider video technology in the identification of bad actors before the attack occurs. As shown clearly in many case studies of terrorist and criminal attacks, a chief concern of the surveillant is "where are the cameras?" An imagary-based collection of surveillance activites assists private organzations in identifying potential preoperational survillance without the need for personal identifiying information (PII)[2] of the subject, where there is not expectation of privacy, therein alleviating the organzation of the extensive laws and policies that are in place to protect such information inside the United States. The United Kingdom, for instance, has upgraded the Data Protection Act 1998 to state if a person "is recognizable" then it is "personal data" and formal requests can be made by the subject to review such data.[3]

---

[2] PII is defined in DoD 5400.11-R, Department of Defense Privacy Program, May 14, 2007 as: Personal Information. Information about an individual that identifies, links, relates, or is unique to, or describes him or her, for example, a social security number; age; military rank; civilian grade; marital status; race; salary; home phone numbers; or other demographic, biometric, personnel, medical, and financial information. Such information is also known as personally identifiable information (i.e., information that can be used to distinguish or trace an individual's identity, such as their name, social security number, date and place of birth, mother's maiden name, and biometric records, including any other personal information that is linked or linkable to a specified individual).

[3] legislation.gov.uk

4.3 Surveillance Detection on the Horizon

As of now, there is a lack of ability to respond to information from the multitude of cameras in real time, but that is being changed through behavioral recognition and almost unbelievably fast facial recognition software. The surveillance market is estimated to reach $3.2 billion by 2016[4] and shows no sign of dissolving over the next decade.

However, until AI surpasses the human ability of cognition and microbehavioral identification, human beings are the most valuable receptors for identifying threating and/or suspicious actors.

Surveillance detection is increasingly becoming a known and valued methodology. Security designers will begin to incorporate surveillance and threat detection into the overall security design of facilities. A thoughtful thesis from the Naval Post Graduate School[5] utilized problematic matrixes and zero-sum models to conclude that a protected facility increases its opportunity to catch the bad guy in the act by (1) reducing the number of entrances into a facility and (2) increasing the length of time it takes to reach those entrances. Seems security designers will take this into account when involved in facility design.

The development and use of unmanned aerial vehicles (UAVs) on the battlefield have

[4] Homeland Security Research Corp.
[5] *Optimal Randomized Surveillance Patterns to Detect Intruders Approaching a Military Installation*, Trevor D. McLemore, Ensign, U.S. Navy B.S. United States Naval Academy, 2006.

already begun to cross into the public and private sector. The laws for these surveillance platforms have not kept pace with the technologies and capabilities. With that said, the integration of ground operators into a command center that receives UAV feeds—all in the name of threat detection—is a work in progress, particularly for special events (such as World Cup, Olympics, and marathons) that require an elevated response to threat in real time.

Sensor systems, involving high-resolution cameras and global positioning devices attached to space-based telescopes, aircraft, balloons, unmanned drones, explorers, and probes of all types, are now widely used to detect the electromagnetic spectrum of the planet's resources in most wavelengths—optical, infrared, ultraviolet, radio, etc. The results are used to feed data to Web-based or smartphone apps for analysis covering weather forecasts, disaster interventions, animal distribution, ecosystem health, 24-hour communications, and video news footage.

With military networks, satellites track the world's most secret military and government installations and test sites using software that enables surveillance of the remotest areas on the planet. This information is also used for research, using images from Google Earth satellite maps to replace traditional archaeological methods, by governments to monitor border integrity, and by nongovernmental organizations(NGOs) to safeguard wildlife against poaching in protected areas. Powerful probes and remote autonomous vehicle landers are used increasingly in space exploration to obtain fly-by views of planets, moons, asteroids, and, in the future, mining options.

Drones/UAVs are likely to become common in the future, sharing airspace with piloted aircraft. They are currently used for surveillance spying and kill missions, but in the future will be used for reconnaissance by most governments, NGOs, and private corporations.

They can monitor a range of information sources, vastly reducing the operational risk in conflict areas and allowing surveillance by sensors that can record full-motion video, infrared patterns, radio, and mobile phone signals. They can also refuel on remote short airstrips, extending effective air range by thousands of kilometers.

Next-gen drones will be autonomous and smaller, able to navigate, and eventually make target decisions, controlled by complex algorithms and Web feeds, eliminating human operators from the decision loop entirely (Figure 4.2). They will be used by every type of organization: criminal networks, private security

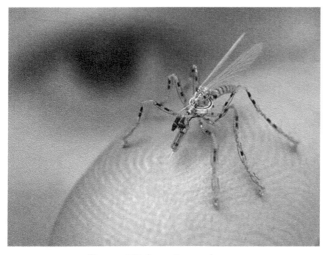

Figure 4.2 A next-gen drone.

businesses, NGOs, and social activist groups, providing a variety of logistical, security, news gathering, and research services.

However, many legal, ethical, and regulatory issues remain to be resolved before UAVs will be able to operate in lockstep with human-controlled vehicles. There is now fierce push-back by the community against another method of individual privacy invasion.

Threat detection programs have increasingly begun to be incorporated into the holistic security apparatus. By combining highly specialized threat detection agents with CCTV behavioral recognition software, in culmination with suspicious activity reporting systems that gather, collate, and analysis threat patterns, in addition to UAV-persistent surveillance capabilities, the world of reactive policing and counterterrorism will lean much more toward proactive capabilities that can and will stop criminals and terrorists *before* they strike.

GLOSSARY

Actionable information: Information directly useful to customers for immediate exploitation without having to go through the full intelligence production process.

Counterintelligence: Organized activity of an intelligence service designed to block an enemy's sources of information, to deceive the enemy, to prevent sabotage, and to gather political and military information.

Countersurveillance: All measures, active or passive, taken to counteract hostile surveillance.

Counterterrorism: Action or strategy intended to counteract or suppress terrorism.

Criminal: An individual who breaks the law.

Criminal enterprise: All illegal activity committed.

C-Suite: The executive level of a company with the CEO, CFO, CIO, etc.

Dope-on-a-rope: Informant.

Emotionally disturbed persons: Individuals found within an administrative site, assessed as either temporarily or permanently psychologically or mentally impaired to a degree that the person is gravely disabled or presents a clear danger to that person or another.

Espionage: The gathering of intelligence by state-sponsored agents.

Foreign intelligence entity: Any foreign organization, person, or group (public, private, or governmental) that conducts intelligence activities to acquire U.S. information, block or impair U.S. intelligence collection, influence U.S. policy, or disrupt U.S. systems and programs. This term includes a foreign intelligence and security service.

Hostile civil disturbance entities: Identified organizations known to target Department of Defense personnel, facilities, and assets through violence and other destructive and disruptive means.

HSL: Hostile surveillance zone

HVL: High-value target

IED: Improvised explosive device

Illegal imaging: The act of taking photos or recording video footage without prior authorization as outlined in jurisdictional law.

Intelligence: Information of a political or military value.

Measuring: Actively measuring distances of physical locations or objects by individuals located at that site through simple pacing, ground still photography, and/or commercially obtained overhead still photography. Measuring is a key step in the planning phase of attack/exploitation cycles, as the collection of such information assures the accuracy of plans, logistics, and execution.

NJTTF: National Joint Terrorism Task Force

Observation: Also regarded as "physical surveillance," this is a systematic and deliberate observation of a person by any means on a continuing basis or the acquisition of a nonpublic communication by a person not a party thereto or visibly present thereat through any means not involving electronic surveillance.

Operational Security (OPSEC): A protective and proactive discipline implemented to mitigate the risk of inadvertent exposure of personnel, methods, and means falling under surveillance detection (SD) purview. SD ensures and manages the continuous implementation of this discipline as to safeguard assigned personnel from potential negative or lethal actions having terrorism, antigovernment, foreign intelligence, and/or criminal nexus.

Presidential Executive Order 12333: President Ronald Reagan signed Presidential Executive Order 12333 on December 4, 1981 (U.S. President 1981, 1). The directive delineated the duties and responsibilities of the various U.S. intelligence agencies. This directive was also designed to protect the United States, its national interests and citizens, from foreign security threats. It also prohibited assassinations by stating, "No person employed by or acting on behalf of the United States Government shall engage in, or conspire to engage in, assassination" (U.S. President 1981, 18).

Perch: A specific location within an HSL, usually elevated.

Querying: Also referred to as elicitation; the acquisition of information from a person or group in a manner that does not disclose the intent of the interview or conversation. A technique of human source intelligence collection, generally overt, unless the collector is other than he or she purports to be.

RAM: Random antiterrorist measure

Red zone: A dedicated HSL.

SAR: Suspicious activity reporting process

SCIF: Secret Compartmental Information Facility

See Something, Say Something: A public access program for individual reporting of suspicious activity to law enforcement.

Surveillance: The systematic observation of aerospace, surface, or subsurface areas, places, persons, or things by visual, aural, electronic, photographic, or other means.

Surveillance detection: Measures taken to detect and/or verify whether an individual, vehicle, or location is under surveillance.

Surveillant: An individual who conducts surveillance.

Suspicious activity (SA): Observed behavior indicative of criminal activities, intelligence gathering, or other preoperational planning related to national security or public safety.

Terrorism: The unlawful use of violence or threat of violence to instill fear and coerce governments and/or societies. Terrorism is often motivated by religious, political, or other ideological beliefs and is committed in the pursuit of goals that are usually political.

Terrorist: An individual who plans or executes criminal violence in pursuit of a political agenda.

Terrorist-related suspicious activity: Observed behavior consistent with preoperational targeting relating to a potential terrorist threat(s) to national security interests. Furthermore, any activity or behavior related to planning, preparation (including probes), and attack execution.

Test of security: Any attempt to measure reaction times and actions by police, security personnel, and/or other first responders. A supposedly simple mistake such as a vehicle approaching a security barrier and then turning around or an attempt to circumvent access control procedures in order to assess strengths and weaknesses of police and equipment can disguise acts of test of security.

Threat: An entity or action that plans to cause injury and/or damage.

Threat detection: The actions and processes to identify, detect, and classify a threat.

Three-letter agency: Jargon for federal agencies such as FBI, CIA, NSA, DHS, and DOJ.

Timing: A subset of observation or "physical surveillance" with the intent of identifying the precise moment in which gaps of security appear; associated patterns of life or reoccurring patterns set by individuals of interest, assets, and critical mission functions. Adversarial planners require this information in support of the analysis, collection management, and dissemination targeting cycle.

TMU: Threat management unit

Tradecraft: Techniques of surveillance and countersurveillance.

TTPs: Techniques, tactics, and procedures

VBIED: Vehicle-borne improvised explosive device (car bomb).

INDEX

Note: Page numbers with "*b*" denote boxes; "*f*" figures.

Printed and bound by CPI Group (UK) Ltd, Croydon, CR0 4YY

03/10/2024

01040422-0005